WATCHING POLITICIANS
Essays on Participant Observation

WATCHING POLITICIANS
Essays on Participant Observation

RICHARD F. FENNO, JR.

IGS Press
Institute of Governmental Studies
University of California at Berkeley
1990

Library of Congress Cataloging-in-Publication Data

Fenno, Richard F., 1926-
    Watching politicians : essays on participant observation / Richard F. Fenno, Jr.
        p. cm.
    Includes bibliographical references.
    ISBN 0-87772-323-0
    1. Political science--Research--United States. 2. Politicians--Research--United
States. 3. Political scientists--United States. 4. Participant observation. 5. Quayle,
Dan, 1947- . I. Title.
JA88.U6F46   1990
324'.0724--dc20   89-26974
                                               CIP

CONTENTS

Foreword

For the last quarter century, those of us who teach American politics and government have had the benefit of an extraordinary resource in the work of Richard F. Fenno, Jr. He has spent enormous amounts of time and energy watching and listening to members of Congress in their native habitat—Capitol Hill and their home districts. He has recorded with great fidelity and sensitivity the sights and sounds that surround members of Congress and that are made by members of Congress—rather as Jane Goodall has done with her no less distinctive population of primates.

Professor Fenno has gone beyond the recording of field-work observations; he has thought about what he has seen and experienced, and has shaped these thoughts into the sorts of persuasive arguments that have helped a generation of scholars and students of Congress, other legislative bodies, and political institutions more generally to see more clearly how these institutions are put together, how they get their work done, how they provide incentives that guide the behavior of their inhabitants, how they accommodate to the political ambitions of their members and express the varied views of public policy they espouse. Over the 200 years that there has been a Congress of the United States, the foremost body of scholarly work that helps us understand that institution is the work created by Richard Fenno. In the process of creating that body of work, he has been an inspiration to his colleagues, a devoted and imaginative teacher, and a thoughtful and generous friend of the scholarly enterprise. This has, of course, vastly expanded his intellectual influence, and has tended to elevate the standards of inquiry where his influence has spread.

Scholars and professional students of American government at the University of California at Berkeley were particularly pleased when he agreed to visit with us and to give a series of Jefferson Lectures. These lectures resulted from reflections on the coincidence that one of the members of Congress he chose to study some years ago—a young senator named Dan Quayle—was unexpectedly selected to become a candidate for the vice presidency of the United States. For the first time in his life Quayle received public scrutiny of quite a different sort than that undertaken by a scholar. Fenno watched the discovery of Quayle by the mass media from the unique perspective of someone who had himself studied Quayle, as well as other politicians, for years. Dan Quayle's sudden fame prompted Fenno to think about the different ways people differently situated—other politicians, journalists, scholars—see politicians at work.

Needless to say, these ruminations made for a fascinating set of lectures. In addition, the lectures resonated strongly with other writings of his in which Fenno has discussed the strategies and tactics and etiquette of empirical field work. We thought that it would be a service to scholars and other students of politics if we were to publish all of Fenno's methodological writings in one place. Thus, we hope to add to the literature an important statement on the theory and practice of watching politicians.

Fenno is a past president of the American Political Science Association, a member of the American Academy of Arts and Sciences and—rather remarkably for a political scientist—a member of the National Academy of Sciences. His books are all classic and definitive works. To recite some of their names is to give a list of the best works there are on their respective subjects: *The President's Cabinet* (1959); *The Power of the Purse* (1966); *Congressmen in Committees* (1973); *Home Style: House Members in Their Districts* (1978); and, most recently, *The Making of a Senator: Dan Quayle* (1989). Since 1957 he has taught at the University of Rochester, where he is University Distinguished Professor and Kenan Professor of Political Science.

Nelson W. Polsby
Institute of Governmental Studies
University of California at Berkeley

Preface

This book grew out of the Jefferson Lectures given at the University of California at Berkeley in the spring of 1989. The lectures themselves grew out of my experiences with a manuscript—later, a book—about Dan Quayle as a United States senator. I had been talking to politicians for 30 years and accompanying them while they worked for 20 years; and the Quayle manuscript had been written from this interview-plus-personal-observation perspective. My post-research experiences with it, I believed, were sufficiently new and sufficiently consequential to warrant the interest of others who study politicians at close range. Or those who think about the contribution made by this kind of research to political science.

Since I had spoken and written about this general subject on several previous occasions, Nelson W. Polsby, Director of UC Berkeley's Institute of Governmental Studies, suggested that the Jefferson Lectures might be packaged with some of the earlier commentaries. This book is the result. It represents a collection of one person's experience and ruminations on observation-based research on politicians. All but Chapter Three were delivered as lectures. The Jefferson Lectures are to be found in Chapters One and Two.

These first two chapters consist of my 1989 reflections on the Quayle manuscript, as it posed problems for a political scientist and as its subject matter was treated by journalists during the 1988 presidential campaign. They form the centerpiece of the book. They are accompanied by material produced in the years between 1978 and 1988. The Introduction is an advocacy paper; it argues the need for more observational research on politicians. Chapter Three describes the participant observation research method, its conduct and its problems, in considerable detail. It recounts several years of experience travelling with 18 members of the House of Representatives in their home districts. As my baseline methodological essay, it provides essential background for the discussion of my relationship with Dan Quayle in Chapters One and Two.

This methodological essay is followed by two chapters, which combine advocacy with an extended example. One takes off from the dependence of congressional leaders on the knowledge they have of their followers and presents the case study of one typically anonymous member of the House to illustrate how much stimulation political scientists might derive from knowledge about a single ordinary politician. The final chapter argues that participant observation sensitizes the researcher to matters of context and sequence; and it examines decision making by six senators on the same legislation in order to explicate the relevance of these two ideas for describing and for theorizing.

I have no desire, here, to produce further reflections on reflections. The essays speak for themselves. But they are not intended to define the farthest reaches or the most important contributions of participant observation as a method of research. People with more knowledge, more imagination, and a surer sense for what other political scientists really need, can do that. These essays are in the nature of a first cut at finding a place for observational research in the political science enterprise. They reflect a strong belief that such research can help and a strong desire to be of help. They reflect the conviction that it is a kind of research that is hard to discipline, and they embody suggestions for achieving that discipline. They also reflect the notion that participant observers are perfectly entitled to do a little theorizing on their own; and they seek to encourage that activity. The essays assume that if participant observation research is done well, the method will find a secure place in a political science that explains politics.

For those who tell me, from time to time, that this kind of research is not participant observation, because it lacks the total involvement of an internship or employment on a politician's staff, these essays might allay criticism. I surely agree that the method is more observation than it is participation. But it is not simply a matter of talking and watching. When you are constantly in the company of a politician for several working days, you discuss interpretations with one another, you do things together, you respond to the same stimuli, you assist one another. There is a dynamic interactive aspect to the relationship that requires, to my mind, the notion of participation. Thankfully, however, we do not have to decide such matters. It is not important what we call it—only that we do it.

I wish to thank my colleagues in the Political Science Department at Rochester for helping me improve my earlier presentation of Chapter One. For their help in monitoring television for Chapter Two, I thank Louise and Jerry Battist, Betty June and Randy Calvert, Sharon and Mark Fenno, Lillian (Kate) Grozier, Kay and Bernard Lynch, Laurie and Irving Spar. At Rochester, I thank Janice Brown for her skillful work with the original notes and manuscripts. At UC Berkeley's Institute of Governmental Studies I thank my longtime friend Nelson Polsby for his encouragement. I also thank Jerry Lubenow for overseeing this project, and Maria Wolf for her editing. Most of all, I thank my silent partner in all these endeavors. She held things together and kept things going.

Introduction

WATCHING POLITICIANS: A RESEARCH PERSPECTIVE[*]

America's elective politicians—in my case members of Congress—are the most talked about and yet the least understood elements of our political system. They are the subject of stories in every daily newspaper and on every nightly television newscast; but they are not the subject of academic research. Of course, this is an exaggeration if one takes into account all the research that has something to do with our politicians. But if one takes into account only those studies based on some personal contact with politicians, it is not an exaggeration. In either case, the proportions of the argument are correct; and it is the matter of proportions that underlies the academic argument for devoting much more attention to elective politicians.

Put more broadly, elective politicians are discussed in the news because they are so crucial to the operation of the political system. Indeed, their election, their presence, their decision making is what makes America a representative democracy. There is, then, a huge mismatch between the central importance of elective politicians to our system of government and their peripheral importance in political science scholarship. One of the reasons for this mismatch is the reluctance and/or the inability of political scientists to observe elective politicians personally and at close range. Political scientists should close that academic distance by undertaking more observation-based research on elective politicians.

Another argument in support of the need for research derives more from the perspective of the citizenry. It is the relationship between elective officials and citizens that is the hallmark of a representative democracy. This relationship is not now a healthy one. For some years, nation-wide polls have registered low, and increasingly lower, levels of citizen trust in government and citizen respect for institutions of government—such as Congress—inhabited by elective politicians. Parents, when asked, do not want their children to pursue careers in elective politics. Negative attitudes of this sort, when widely held, undermine the everyday operation of representative government and threaten its ultimate acceptance by the people to whom it is responsible.

---

[*]Presented at the University of Oklahoma April 14, 1988. Published by permission of *Extensions*, Summer 1988.

Carried to higher levels of government, these attitudes can cause serious disability and breakdown. The Iran-Contra investigation revealed the high cost to our political system when nonelected officials hold elective officials in low regard. The disregard, in some executive circles, for the intentions, values, interests, prerogatives, perspectives and legitimacy of the elective politicians in Congress lies at the heart of the problem. This attitude of disdain, as practiced and expressed at high levels, reflects the negative attitudes expressed, if not practiced, by the citizenry at large. The point is simply that a good deal of negativism toward elective politicians is present throughout the political system, and its presence is not a sign of good health.

Better understanding might have a beneficial effect on the attitudes of citizens toward their elected politicians and hence, improve the health of the political system. The term "citizens" includes not just voters but—even more important—the nonelected officials who work with elective politicians and the media people who interpret the activities of elective politicians. Of course, one cannot predict what, if any, effect more close-in research might have—or on whom.

Whether or not the effects will be beneficial is not known. The present unhealthy relationship between citizens and politicians exists side by side with a knowledge gap, or an understanding gap, on the part of citizens. As the knowledge gap is filled, it is quite likely that a new appreciation of, if not more positive attitudes toward, elective politicians will be inspired. If that does not happen, the present relationship will most likely deteriorate. While the American political system can doubtless withstand a good bit of distrust, disrespect and disregard for its elective politicians, just as surely its tolerance has limits. From that perspective, any prospect for improvement deserves nourishment.

Political scientists ought to learn about politicians by talking to them, watching them and following them around. Some research can be done by bringing politicians—aspiring, active or retired—to the academic work place. But most of it must be done in the setting in which politicians operate, in their natural habitats. The aim is to see the world as they see it, to adopt their vantage point on politics. For it is precisely this view, from over the politician's shoulder, that is now missing from academic research.

Journalists, of course, regularly adopt this perspective. To a large degree, therefore, present-day opinions of elected politicians are those of journalists. That is, up to now, journalists have been doing the work of political scientists. But journalistic interest tends to be episodic rather than sustained; and journalists' writing tends to stress idiosyncracies rather than regularities. (They may also be inclined toward negativism.) If political scientists do not increase and improve their observation, however, they will remain hostage to the views of journalists. That situation, too, seems unsatisfactory and provides another incentive for academics to proceed. The aim is to produce a more complete, more reliable, and more general picture of elective politicians than either academics or journalists have yet produced.

What would our research as political scientists look like? The aim would be to look at both the personal side and the contextual side of the politician's world. On the one hand, we need to incorporate politicians' ambitions, goals, motivations, experiences and values; and on the other hand, we want to investigate the several environments in which they work, both electoral and governmental, in the constituency and at the capitol. We want to learn about how they run for office and how they govern in office. We want to understand the opportunities and the constraints that face them when they act in both settings. We want to understand what they think their job is, and what they think about their job. We want to understand the institutional structures within which and around which they must work, as well as the kinds of people from whom they must learn and with whom they must negotiate.

We want to investigate how and why politicians make their important choices within these various contexts—whether or not to run, how to campaign, which policies to support, which policies to push for, what coalitions to build, what image to present, what privacy to protect, how to spend their time, whom to trust, with whom to incur obligations, what values to uphold, etc. We want to examine the decisions that carry people into elective politics. Are there normal paths the elective politicians follow? If so, what is the logic that propels them along such paths? If not, are people propelled into elective office randomly, by accidental opportunity? If so, what motivates people to seize the opportunity? How important to the decision to seek (or not seek) office are matters like previous experience, circumstances of the moment, family conditions, likelihood of winning, alternative careers, probable support, etc.? This is but a sample of questions political scientists need to answer—for particular politicians, for particular types of politicians, in particular institutional settings at particular points in time.

Finally, political scientists need to find ways to connect their research effort to a complementary teaching effort. What is needed, eventually, is a teaching program that trains people to do the kind of research I am advocating. That means alternating people between immersion in the field and instruction in the classroom. One reason political scientists do so little observational research is because they are not trained to do so and because they believe, therefore, that such research is a less legitimate form of political science than that which is done by manipulating second hand data at a comfortable distance from the real world of politics. But participant observation has a large set of interesting problems—of data, of method, and of ethics—which need to be discussed in conjunction with practice. Only as people actually combine the two, will the kind of research I am advocating take hold as a legitimate enterprise in political science circles.

1

Political Scientists and Politicians: The Dan Quayle Experience

At approximately 5:55 p.m. last August 16th, I was on Cape Cod minding my own business. I had spent six years off and on, from 1980 to 1986, watching and talking to Senator Dan Quayle of Indiana—both in Washington and in his home state. In the summer of 1987, I had completed a case study on Quayle and put it in the drawer. I hoped, later on, to fit that manuscript into a larger book on the United States Senate. I had read in the papers that Quayle was being considered by George Bush to be his vice presidential running mate. I was pleased, because I considered it to be a tip of the hat to a young senator for doing good work in the Senate. But I did not take it seriously.

At 6:00 I turned on the television to watch the news just in time to hear George Bush say, "My choice for the vice presidency is Senator Dan Quayle of Indiana." I was shocked. Almost immediately I broke out in goose bumps. I said to my wife, "Did you hear what I just heard?" She says I turned both white and speechless. My first instinct was to deny the whole thing. I rushed up to the TV and changed channels—on the hunch that it was some kind of mistake, or joke, or parody and that I would find "reality" on another channel. But there it was again. I remained speechless while reality sunk in. The reality was that I had just won the lottery. My life was not going to be the same for some time; and I was about to undergo a series of experiences which, as a political scientist, I had not known before.

Participant Observation

In the most general sense, my Dan Quayle experiences are not new. They are an extension of, or a version of, some earlier ones—in the sense that all of them grow out of the same kind of research. My preferred term for that research is participant observation—by which I mean the practice of gathering data by watching and talking to people in their natural habitats. At the time I won the lottery, I had been engaged in participant observation for nearly 30 years, and I had formulated some ideas about how to do it, why, and with what consequences.

In 1978, after seven years of travelling with members of the United States House of Representatives in their home districts, I set down my ideas on the subject in an appendix to a book called *Home Style: House Members in Their Districts* (see Chapter Three in this book). When I finished, I believed that I had said all I had to say on participant observation. Or to put it another way, I believed I had had all the learning experiences I was going to have, that I had faced all the contingencies I was going to face. I was wrong. My experiences since August 16th have caused me to reflect further on the adequacy of my ideas. What I have to say today, then, can be thought of as an appendix to an appendix.

Of what value, you might ask, is any appendix of this sort? Only this, that participant observation as a research method has distinctive problems. Most of our political science proceeds at a far distance from the everyday life of our politicians. And most of our guidelines for conducting and testing research are written by and for them. But there will always be—I repeat *always* be—some political scientists who will want to close that distance to study politicians at the closest possible range. They will wish to do so for a variety of compelling and durable reasons: because they enjoy politics, because they believe politicians are important, because they want a first-hand exposure to politics and to politicians, and because this mode of research presents a large intellectual challenge.

What guidelines can be produced for them? What can we do to keep this research mode securely anchored within our discipline, while at the same time retaining the juices of everyday politics that are the special attraction of the mode? There are guidelines that can help. But they are far less easy to specify, to follow, and to test than the guidelines set forth in the more quantitative realms of the discipline. Many of them are matters of judgment. Probably, they can only be established by trial and error and by some method of successive approximations.

It is in the nature of discussions of participant observation research that they grow out of experience and tend, therefore, to be anecdotal and idiosyncratic. My reflections today will be no exception to that story-telling—"what I did last summer"—tradition. And I apologize for that in advance. Participant observers go into the field, return to the scholarly community, report their experience, and extrapolate some research rules from that particular experience. These rules tend to be fairly imprecise. And agreement on them—in canonical form anyway—has been hard to come by. On the other hand, as with any other method, practitioners of participant observation do recognize a standard set of methodological and political worries. I shall try to do justice to this more general side of things too.

What made the recent experience different from all earlier ones is that this time most of the problems arose *after* the research had been completed and not while the research was in progress. It was not a problem of how to do the research, but how to cope with certain consequences that flowed from the research. That produced a problem of control over the research product that I had not encountered before. The difference became amply obvious on the evening of August 16th.

My first sober reaction to the news was to treat the event as a providential research opportunity—a chance to travel with the vice presidential nominee during the campaign, a chance to add another chapter to my Quayle manuscript. I moved quickly to get on top of the breaking story. By 6:15 I was making calls to friends and family with VCR's, to ask them to capture for me the evening news and the convention coverage for the rest of the week, on all three major networks. By 6:30, I had a far flung team of research assistants—from Massachusetts to New York—lined up and ready to record. I was, of course, excited—excited for Quayle, excited for the improved prospects for the Quayle segment of the Senate book.

But as I watched the Quayle story unfold on television that first evening, another reaction set in. Almost immediately, it became clear that no one knew anything about Dan Quayle. "My God," I kept saying, "I know more about Dan Quayle than anyone else in the world—and nobody in the world knows I know." It was a weird feeling of disembodiment, sitting there all evening on a 253-page gold mine of information, while the nation's journalists worked from a couple of pages in the *Almanac of American Politics* and scrounged for the tiniest scrap of extra information. But my phone never rang. The incongruity of it all produced considerable agitation as the evening progressed.

On the heels of the question: "What could I do to add to my information on Quayle?" came another question: "What could I do with the information I already had?" The events of the evening began to present themselves not just as a research opportunity but also as a

7

publishing opportunity. Obviously, a large vacuum existed out there, and I was in a better position to fill that vacuum than anyone in the United States. So why shouldn't I? I had little doubt that there would be some public interest in what I had to say. And if I did not say it, wouldn't some investigative journalists eventually dig up the information and say it for me? The idea that my information advantage was only temporary, that the national media would soon catch up dominated my earliest thoughts. Publishing one's "results" before others get the same idea is, after all, among the most elemental of our scholarly instincts.

Thinking about publishing, however, was far more difficult than thinking about doing more research. For there were questions about what to publish, in what form and how soon. For each of these questions, in turn, there was the further question—of the possible consequences for the author, for the manuscript, for Dan Quayle, and even, for the presidential campaign itself.

As I watched the vice presidential story unfold that first evening, I realized that if people knew what I knew, they would not only learn something they didn't know about Dan Quayle, they would learn something *favorable* about him. And he was not getting much favorable attention. The media, I thought, was being unusually hard on someone they did not know. I came quickly to believe, that in the context in which I had been placed, my information was not neutral—that I was in a position to help Dan Quayle, that if I published I *would* help Dan Quayle. What should I do?

While I had never confronted this exact situation before, I had developed a general framework within which to think about the relationship between political scientists and the politicians they study. My general notion was—and is—that political scientists should bend every effort to maintain their personal distance from the politicians they study, and that they should refrain from engaging in any behavior that has the intention of affecting political outcomes. Or to put it in a more positive way, political scientists, should bend every effort to behave as if their only intended audience were their fellow political scientists, and they should conduct their relationships with politicians so as to enhance their professional credibility within the scholarly community.

This general notion assumes a degree of separation between the world of the political scientist and the real world of politics; it assumes that some imaginary *boundary* exists between them. It holds, further, that this boundary should be maintained and, further still, that the matter of boundary maintenance is especially important for political scientists who do participant observation. For we are the ones who work closest to the boundary, who work back and forth across the boundary. We are the ones for whom the opportunities and the incentives to cross over and become political actors, to go into politics, are the strongest and the most omnipresent. For years, for example, I have been asked by people who know what I do but do not understand what I do, why I don't run for office myself. It seems so obvious and natural to them. My notion is that participant observers should resist these nearby temptations. We should cross over into the real political world to collect our data and formulate our hypotheses; but we should come back to write, to publish, and to be evaluated within the world of political science.

Having set forth this framework of ideas, however, it is immediately necessary to concede its ambiguity. The idea of a boundary is totally lacking in definition. At best, we need to think of it as a band and not a line—a border zone, a no-man's-land or whatever—so that crossing is more like a journey than a leap and the point of no return remains highly imprecise. Indeed, everything about participant observation—from the collection of the data to the evaluation of the results is bathed in ambiguity. The variability of personal relationships plus the uncertain effects of time and context insure ambiguity. That is why scholarly agreement on research rules is, in the end, so elusive and hard to come by.

Research rules that involve boundary lines, and prescriptions about behavior in the boundary area are inherently controversial. For they touch upon personal codes of conduct and upon matters of ethics. And there is neither profit nor pleasure in prescribing such codes. Last December, in a speech to the National Press Club, *Washington Post* journalist David Broder prescribed some boundary lines for his colleagues. "There's a real danger," he told them, "in blurring the lines between politicians and journalists...we damn well better make it clear [that] we are not part of a Washington insider clique where politicians, publicists, and journalists are interchangeable parts."[1] His remarks stirred up a good deal of controversy. One part of it was testimony to the difficulty of line drawing.[2] The other part was testimony to the "holier than thou" attack awaiting anyone who tries. "Who anointed Broder...[the] high priest of journalistic ethics," thundered Pat Buchanan. "When did the *Post* start giving holy orders?" And he dismissed Broder as "a sermonizing, sanctimonious prig."[3] I hope to be spared such treatment.

But that is why we produce demurrers such as the one I produced in the original Appendix: "The personal stance I have reported here is only one variant—not better, not worse than others, just more comfortable for

---

[1]David Broder, "Beware the Washington Insider," *Washington Post National Weekly Edition*, December 12-18, 1988.

[2]See Charles Trueheart, "As The Revolving Door Turns," *Washington Post National Weekly Edition*, January 16-22, 1989.

[3]Patrick Buchanan, "Insiders Don't Bother Public–Liberal Bigots Do," *Rochester Democrat and Chronicle*, December 29, 1988. Broder's reply will be found in David Broder, "Thin Skinned Journalists," *Washington Post*, January 11, 1989.

me." Comments like this probably encourage disarray among practitioners and puzzlement among onlookers. But it is hard to do better. For no one wishes to act as legislator, policeman, judge, or censor in dealing with adult colleagues in these matters. Persuasion, example, and open exchange are the only available instruments for bringing about agreement.

My own implementing rules, as set forth in that first Appendix, included such boundary maintaining proscriptions as: join no parties, enlist in no causes, give no interviews, keep the lowest possible public profile, don't stay for long in Washington, don't make personal friends out of politicians. But later experience caused me to give ground. I spent a year in Washington in 1981-82 to observe some senators; and a few years after that, I began to respond to inquiring journalists. On the whole, however, I still held to the general framework and to the implementing rules of thumb when I began my relationship with Senator Dan Quayle in September of 1980—and when I ended it in October of 1986.

In the fall of 1980, you may recall, there were a number of Senate races pitting conservative House members against well known liberal incumbents—in Idaho, South Dakota, Iowa, Wisconsin, and Indiana. And I was looking for a matched pair. I first chose Iowa Senator John Culver as my liberal; and then chose Dan Quayle as my conservative House member—probably because travels with two of its House members for *Home Style* had given me a slight familiarity with Indiana politics. But it was a stab in the dark. I knew nothing about Quayle.

I wrote a letter to him cold turkey; and a staffer responded by telephone—positively but warily. Later, in the campaign files, I came across her subsequent memo to Quayle.

> I have told Mr. Fenno that he is welcome to travel with us on Thursday and that a decision about his travelling Friday will be made by you on Thursday evening. The only drawback that I can see to his continuing on the trail may be his inability to keep up with the pace. However, it may also be advisable to just let him travel Thursday due to the two CCC events. (Conference of Concerned Christians) He seems personable on the telephone. He will be coming from Birmingham where he has just finished reviewing the Senate race there.

The night I arrived, three campaign staffers came to my motel to have a beer and check me out. Apparently, they concluded that I was not too far gone, either physically or spiritually. When I got into the car with Quayle the next morning, he said "How long are you going to be with us?" "Two days if it's okay with you" I said. "Fine" he said. And I ended up staying for three.

For the next six years Dan Quayle remained, as I wrote in my book, "accessible and forthcoming, informative and interested."[4] Our relationship became one of some mutual trust—in which I expected him to be open with me, and he expected me to be fair to him. It was a nearly ideal research relationship between political scientist and politician—the more noteworthy, perhaps, because the senator's natural affinities did not run to the academic community. It lasted for six years, through four more visits in Indiana and a year of monitoring his activity in Washington—through 20 odd hours of one-on-one conversation, and four times that many hours of close-in observation.

In the *Home Style* Appendix I had written that,

> sometimes...a professional relationship threatens to slide into a personal friendship.... I worried about it and tried to guard against it. I did not want them as friends—only respondents.... Some members became friends. But they remained business friends rather than personal friends, social friends, or family friends.

That is the kind of professional relationship I thought I had established with Dan Quayle when I left him in October 1986. Yet, when he appeared on the TV screen with Bush, I had immediately gotten goose bumps. They were not goose bumps for my country. Nor were they goose bumps for my manuscript. They came from the sudden thrill of having someone with whom I had spent a lot of time nominated to be vice president of the United States. (Those of you who have had someone you know pretty well nominated for vice president will know exactly how I felt!) In 25 years of hanging around politicians I had never had goose bumps before. It was an emotional reaction, and it signalled an emotional tie to Dan Quayle I had not known I had—one I thought I had carefully guarded against. It was an important discovery for me, but also important for political science. I had discovered the goose bumps test of significance.

Like the goose bumps, my early emotions related to Dan Quayle as a human being—not as a political candidate but as a person. It wasn't that I thought he was a good choice. I did not. Like everyone else, I wondered why George Bush had picked so unseasoned a running mate. Dan Quayle was, simply, someone who had been kind to me, who had helped me with my work, with whom I had shared many experiences, with whom access and rapport had been easily achieved and easily maintained—someone I had gotten to know and gotten to like. Suddenly and unexpectedly, he had been given a chance to reach the very pinnacle of his profession. And I resonated to his good fortune.

---

[4]Richard F. Fenno, Jr., *The Making of A Senator: Dan Quayle*, Washington: CQ Press, 1988, Preface.

By the end of the first evening, this simple goose bump emotion had grown into a sturdier one. That is, I wanted him to do well. By the time he held his first press conference the next morning, there was no doubt that I was rooting for him to perform well and to survive his first media test. Again, it was not that I agreed with him politically or that I wanted him to win. I don't suppose I agreed with him on the issues more than 20 percent of the time. But ideology was no more relevant here than it had been in achieving access and rapport in the beginning. Out in the field, human reactions matter, not ideological ones. Now, too, I just wanted him to give a good public accounting of himself. It was not a politically relevant emotion. Not yet anyway.

But it had a lot of potential for becoming one. And quickly, too, because certain political dimensions of the situation had become pretty clear by the end of the first evening. The media's initial reaction to the nominee was not flattering. They expressed puzzlement as to why he had been chosen; and they questioned his qualifications. The manuscript in my drawer, on the other hand, credited Quayle with a substantial legislative accomplishment, i.e., his start-to-finish leadership in the passage of the Joint Training Partnership Act of 1982. With each passing day of the convention, Quayle's need for help increased. His Wednesday press conference did not go well for him. His compensating efforts in the network anchor booths that evening did not go well either. By Thursday, he was embroiled in controversy and was being showered with adverse publicity. There was even talk of dropping him from the ticket.

As his difficulties increased, so did my emotional involvement. Notes I took on Wednesday evening say, "Now I am upset and feeling very sorry for Quayle. I can't control the emotion. It has taken over from the excitement of last night.... I'm feeling sick to my stomach about what's happening to him." Thursday evening, I wrote "I felt rotten all day. I didn't even want to read the paper. The [Boston] *Globe* is killing him."

For 25 years, I had tried to avoid the kind of emotional entanglements with politicians that would drag me over the boundary and into politics. Now, I was getting very close. Friday night, my notes read: "I feel like I want to help him. But I know I shouldn't. So I'm paralyzed." I was, indeed, suspended between the fundamentals of a political scientist's framework, which told me to stay out of it, and the tug of a personal emotion, which was pulling me into it.

Intervention

Only once before had I faced a boundary line entanglement similar to this one. I had alluded to it in my *Home Style* Appendix:

> In one bizarre set of circumstances...I became involved in the
> campaign of my oldest and closest congressional friend. I

had no effect on the electoral outcome, but I became an intimate for the duration of the campaign; and in the process I abandoned all social science activity. Luckily I had nearly completed my research in that district.

I want to digress for a moment to discuss that first interventionist dilemma, because I think it sheds light on the second one. The House member involved, Barber Conable, Republican of New York, had been my congressman for 10 years, during which time we had seen each other fairly often in both research and nonresearch contexts. He had become by far my most valued participant analyst of legislative life; and he had become an irreplaceable source of my access to other important people on Capitol Hill. His office had become my information center and my home away from home when I worked in Washington. He was not only, to my mind, a crucial scholarly resource; he was the only legislator who had ever become more than a business friend. So there was a personal and emotional, as well as a scholarly attachment to him.

In 1974, that best of all Democratic years, his first "quality challenger"—a very popular female vice mayor of Rochester—announced for the seat. When I returned from Cape Cod in August I learned that two members of my department had signed on to manage her campaign—one as campaign manager and one as pollster. As soon as they saw me, they reported excitedly that their polls indicated that Barber Conable was in trouble. Since his election in 1964, he had had four sleepy reelections without serious opposition; he had no organization left; his supporters were not energized; and his challenger was scoring points by portraying him as someone who was addicted to Washington and had lost touch with the folks back home.

The bizarre aspect of this situation was that two of my own colleagues were working day and night to accomplish something that, I believed, would do severe damage to my research. I did not believe that it was intentional on their part. Or they would not have spoken so openly of their strong desire to bring about Conable's demise. They were certainly aware that I had a good relationship with him; but they had, I assumed, no awareness of its crucial importance to my scholarship. But whatever their state of mind, their involvement was threatening me with extreme scholarly harm. And there was nothing I could say to them.

The question facing me was what else, if anything, to do about it. I could sit on the sidelines, as I had always done, and let nature take its course. Or, I could intervene to affect the outcome. I thought it likely that Conable would win; but it was not a sure thing. I entertained all the electoral doubts that candidates inevitably do. If there was anything I could do to help him win, I believed I had to do it—for I could not accept the risk of losing so valued a research resource. Besides which, having the masterminds of the threat so close to home stimulated my adrenaline and put me in a retaliatory, don't-surrender-without-a-fight mood. Besides which, I did not want to see a friend defeated. I decided to intervene, and I entered into an undeclared war—a gentleman's war—both to protect my scholarly territory and to help reelect a friend.

As soon as I heard my colleagues' prognosis, I called Conable's campaign manager. He said, "I can't get Barber to come home and campaign. You had better call him yourself." I called Conable's home in Washington, related the poll results, and told him: "You're in trouble, you get your tail up here and start campaigning, now." When he protested he had legislative matters to tend to, I said, "I mean now, Barber, now!" He dropped everything and came, saying that "I know I'm in the fight of my life." He stayed for the duration and he campaigned hard. By example, he energized his supporters, and they brought an organization to life. We won 57 percent of the vote. I say we because I had been totally involved emotionally. I had acted intentionally so as to affect the outcome. And to some small degree, I believe I had affected the process, if not the outcome. Whether I did or not is beside the point. I had tried. And the decision to intervene had violated all my participant observer guidelines.

The conditions under which the decision was taken were bizarre. But the decision was the product of two factors that may well be constants—and as such demand special scrutiny. They are professional protection and personal attachment. One generalization about them may be that when professional and personal considerations combine to pull a researcher over the line, boundary maintenance will be maximally difficult. And another may be that when any such pulls arise, the researcher ought to weigh carefully the effects of intervention on the maintenance of his or her own research and act to protect it. No one ought to be expected to accept scholarly suicide if that seems likely to be the price of nonintervention. Ironically, my intervention changed forever my relationship with Barber Conable, but not in ways I had anticipated. He never forgot that telephone call. And I became, in his eyes, an ally who had stood with him in his toughest election fight. The personal relationship between us became too close to be professional. Having entered the fray and won, I had paradoxically lost the very scholarly resource I had sought to protect. Having crossed over the boundary as wholeheartedly as I did, I could not return. And therein, I suppose lies a caution. I could not and did not do any more research on Barber Conable.

The bizarre qualities of the Conable case produced another caution. Participant observers cannot take for granted that our political science colleagues understand the working relationships with politicians on which this research mode depends or the large personal investment that is involved in securing those relationships.

I suppose that the most important caution I should have taken away from that experience was how difficult it is to apply professional absolutes to specific cases. But in the *Home Style* Appendix it was treated as an exception not likely to arise again. And I continued to think of it that way until the Quayle experience taught me otherwise. As I thought about what to do with my Quayle manuscript during convention week, I faced a similar, interventionist dilemma, and the same big question: Should I or should I not act intentionally to affect an outcome in the political world? The clear answer, according to my established guidelines, was the same: No. But there existed, again, complicating personal and professional factors. In the Quayle case, as I have indicated, the personal factor emerged first.

Dan Quayle and I had never been more than business friends. I had left him in October 1986 wanting him to win—as I always had wanted my respondents to win—but as a minimal emotional commitment I would monitor from afar. And I had not seen him since. Nonetheless, my desire to help him grew exponentially as he began to receive what I believed—on the basis of the manuscript—was incomplete and therefore unbalanced media treatment. I believed that I was in a position to help him by redressing the balance. I had no good estimate of Quayle's chances of winning. But I thought, as in the Conable case, that I might have an effect on the process if not the outcome of the campaign. On emotional grounds I grew increasingly disposed to do so.

But there were professional considerations here, too. It was not that Quayle, like Conable, held a special key to my scholarly research. It was that intervention meant publication; and publication would mean widespread public notice; and widespread public notice would bring consequences far beyond anything imagined in the highly localized Conable intervention.

By the end of the first evening, August 16th, I had decided that I could not leave the manuscript in the drawer as if nothing had happened, that something extraordinary had happened, and that I had been presented with an opportunity to publish something that would attract widespread interest. I could add to my research later if I wished. But as scholars, we are in the business of communicating what we know; and I wanted to communicate what I knew. I also wanted to get timely credit for it.

I spent the next several days canvassing the possibilities. "You won't believe this" I would say to potential publishers, "but I'm sitting on a finished 253 page manuscript on...Dan Quayle." It was a guaranteed attention-getter. Having decided to publish, my first thought was to do so as quickly as possible. And I got lots of encouragement. If that meant injecting my information into the campaign blood stream and giving Quayle a timely transfusion, well, that was fine, too. My motives were a mixture of "right the wrong" being done to poor Dan Quayle, and "let people know what you know." The temptation to cross the boundary and intervene in the real political world was strong and growing.

But my canvassing began to reveal how severe the professional costs of publication would be. Fastback publishers, needing a large sale to offset increased printing costs, wanted me to update the manuscript to include such matters of current concern as his National Guard decision, his Paula Parkinson involvement and his academic performance in college. Regular publishers, on the other hand, wanted me to research the vice presidential campaign, to add a chapter on that event, and to publish when the election was over. Magazine editors suggested publishing excerpts from the manuscript; and a national newspaper wanted to send a reporter straightaway to Cape Cod for an in-depth interview. In every case, the manuscript in the desk drawer would have to be changed. Timeliness, it appeared, could be achieved but only at the cost of altering the manuscript.

Canvassing the alternatives helped demonstrate the value of the existing manuscript—that it contained a completed description and a settled judgment totally unaffected by anything that had happened or would happen after the summer of 1987. If I added to it or subtracted from it, its essential unity would be destroyed. The integrity of the analysis, the objectivity of it as far as the vice presidential situation was concerned, the separation of it from the campaign gave it special credibility, and, therefore, a special persuasiveness to anyone who read it. If, on the other hand, I tampered with what I had written in any way, I could easily be written off as having nonscholarly motives—of purposely injecting some fresh, campaign-related bias, be it favorable or unfavorable to Quayle.

Under those circumstances, the manuscript would be treated as a campaign document and cause my fellow political scientists to lose interest in it. The more I thought about it, the clearer it became that no matter what I published, the injection of any part of my analysis into the campaign would cause the entire manuscript to become hopelessly politicized, as people took from it whatever suited their immediate partisan purposes. I would lose all control over the case study and lose professional credibility in the process. The manuscript would never receive a respectful, fair hearing as a political science effort. It was, after all, a political science manuscript. And I wanted it to be evaluated by political scientists. Thus, did an early desire to get it out quickly, give way to a determination to get it out intact.

With this altered set of priorities, I offered it to CQ Press with the stipulation that they publish the manuscript as it had been written in 1987, without change. They agreed, and within their organization, the project got dubbed "operation purity." Two months after we signed the contract, the book was published.

The decision to publish with CQ meant that the book would not be published until after the campaign. Which meant that I had to decide how to behave during the campaign. The line of argument that had led me not to intervene with a manuscript led inexorably, it seemed to me, to a decision to keep all of its contents out of the campaign. And the logic of that decision dictated that I, too, should remain outside the campaign. For anything I said would, in effect, inject the manuscript into the campaign piecemeal and would be mauled by the campaigners. So the decision to publish with CQ carried the corollary decisions to stay out of the campaign altogether, not to try and affect it, not to do research on the campaign, and not to help Dan Quayle.

A half dozen or so journalists—who learned about the manuscript—called for interviews. Some argued that it was my civic duty to tell what I knew; others argued I had an obligation to reassure the country; others argued that it was in my interest to get my name in their paper. I turned them all down. At that point, both my duty and my interest, I believed, ran to the political science community. For 10 weeks, I refused to talk about Dan Quayle or about the contents of my manuscript; and to my knowledge no public word of it—or me—surfaced until well after the election was over. For the duration, at least, I remained on the political science side of the boundary.

The actual decision to intervene was different in the Conable and Quayle cases. Taken together, however, both cases highlight the importance of professional and emotional components in making these decisions. On the professional side, I acted in both cases to maintain the integrity of my research. And I like to think that professional considerations were at least necessary if not sufficient in both decisions. I believe, anyway, that the protection of our scholarship and, hence, our credibility ought to weigh most heavily in our interventionist decisions. For it is the very essence of the political scientist-politician relationship I have advocated that the relationship with our fellow political scientists should remain uppermost in our minds as we do research on real world politicians. Our business is to generalize about the political world—to go out and report back—for the benefit of our colleagues who never go there. If we are to be helpful to them, however, they must be willing to accept our descriptions and to invest in our hypotheses, which they will do only if they find our work credible. And they will, I believe, find us credible to the degree that we follow guidelines that emphasize our separateness from the political world, our boundary problems, and our self-conscious efforts at boundary maintenance.

Whether or not the rest of the world will appreciate, much less honor these prescriptions for professional integrity, however, remains highly problematical. When the Quayle book was published, one of my earliest reviews came in the form of a postcard from a woman who wrote "Dear

Fenno, How much were you paid to write your PR hype book on Quayle? You have lost your integrity and will be remembered as a liar and the ass-kisser of the decade." So I have not been spared. Dave Broder has his Pat Buchanan of Washington, D.C.; I have the critic from Elizabeth, New Jersey.

On the emotional side of things, both cases indicate that there is more emotion embedded in our relationships with the politicians we study than we normally recognize. The Conable decision followed the path of personal attachment; the Quayle decision did not. But the course of the Quayle decision revealed plenty of emotion—enough to cause us worry even as we write up our research. If I look back, for instance, and ask myself, Could I have hurt Dan Quayle if I had included certain comments of his that remain, still unused, in my notes, the answer is "yes." Did I do this for research reasons—as I believed? Or, for prudential reasons—as I also believed? Or for emotional reasons—as I did not believe? My ultimate answer is that I believe the book is fair to Dan Quayle—that I did not go out of my way to tear him down or puff him up. His own comment was that "I think you did a fair job—warts and all." I hope political scientists will concur. But these questions only underscore the importance of keeping the emotional component of the political scientist-politician relationship continuously open for inspection—and for worry.

The decision to stay out of the 1988 campaign proved that observing a vow of chastity does not mean the elimination of emotion. And campaign time is inevitably a time of heightened emotion. By refusing to discuss or examine or even entertain privately any preferences as to the election outcome, I managed to bank my emotions and my preferences until about three weeks before election day. At which point I realized (or admitted) that I did, indeed, have a preference. I wanted the Bush-Quayle ticket to win. I faced the fact that I had spent much of my adult life—increasingly so in recent years—trying to convince members of my profession of the value of participant observation research. My good luck in the lottery had handed me a golden opportunity to put this kind of research on public display. What better chance to make my case? Did I want the largest possible audience for a piece of participant-observation research? Of course I did. And it was obvious that I would sell more books if the Bush-Quayle ticket won. I must have been nuts, I thought, to believe I could stay neutral. Of course, I wanted Dan Quayle to become vice president of the United States.

The final weeks of the campaign were agonizingly long. They were especially agonizing because—true to my rules of disengagement—I kept my strong preference to myself. Dukakis campaigners even came to discuss their vice presidential poll results with me, to ask my advice on whether they should step up their attack on Quayle. Everyone who knew I had a manuscript felt bound to tell me the latest Quayle joke, the implicit assumption being that while I had won the lottery, surely I could not be rooting for someone like that to win. I took all this as something of a compliment—that others believed I would be observing all my strictures against emotional entanglements, that I was as neutral in private as I was in public. But the jokes—with their implication that the person in whom I had invested so heavily, was not worth it—became less and less funny. Privately, I had gone over the boundary with all the enthusiasm of the Conable adventure. For the time being I had completely entangled my life with that of the vice presidential nominee, my career with his. Except while at home, however, I kept all this to myself. It remained a distinctly private emotion—a more mature, more ulcerating form of the goose bumps.

Aftermath

On November 8th, I became the possessor of a soon-to-be-published manuscript about the new vice president of the United States. And I began to take stock of my post-election relationship with him. The manuscript was both an accident and an anomaly. It was not supposed to be a book. It was not written for beyond-the-classroom consumption. It was certainly not written to launch the public life of a new vice president. As a political science book it was nothing special—just a garden variety case study, which would, I hoped, showcase the participant observation style of research. But it had been dropped into a political context that guaranteed an abnormal degree of interest. And all because of one simple feature—completely new to my work. It named names—that is, the new vice president's name.

The book was filled with Dan Quayle's interview comments, Dan Quayle's actions, opinions about Dan Quayle. He had been denied the anonymity with which I had heretofore shielded all the politicians about whom I had written. Barber Conable, had been represented in *Home Style* by a letter of the alphabet—nothing more. But in this book, Dan Quayle would be Dan Quayle. Naming names gives a bite to the writing that encourages publishers to think about audiences beyond the confines of political science. That was, of course, why I thought early publication would help him. And that was why there was cause to wonder about my relationship with him afterward. It was one more new post-research, boundary problem to confront.

In my original appendix, I had set forth a stern anonymity rule:
> If there were any way that I could have "named names" in the book without destroying my access and without jeopardizing the access of future political scientists, I would have done so. It would have given the book's ideas a much wider national audience than they will ever get, attached as

19

they now are, antiseptically, to Representatives A, B, C. But
it could not be done.

The rule sought to recognize our total dependence on the good will of the politicians we study, together with their longevity in office. It was designed to minimize the chance that short run decisions would jeopardize long term accessibility. But it was a rule I had to give up without a struggle once I decided to write in-depth case studies of individual senators. For better or worse, there was no way to cloak them in anonymity. Like my prescriptions about living in Washington or granting interviews, another rule had given way in the face of experience.

My revised rule, which I communicated to my Senate respondents, was that they would be given a chance to review my manuscript prior to publication. I made no promises as to what I would do. But it was my intention to modify or remove objectionable parts, providing they were neither extensive nor crucial to my interpretation. Except for comments I had on tape—and those were a tiny fraction of the total—I could not swear to the total accuracy of every word. I had no interest in writing something they would consider grossly unfair. And in any case, I believed it would be an abuse of their trust to write a story that would do them serious harm.

Pursuant to this revised rule, my first call Wednesday morning after Bush's surprise pick went to Quayle's Senate office to arrange for him to check my manuscript. There was, at that time, a secret copy of it locked in the desk drawer of his top legislative assistant. In May, I had sent the aide a copy to check for errors in my legislative chronicle. After he read it, he had said "Why don't you show it to Dan?" I had asked him what he thought Dan would say. "He'd say publish it. There might be one or two comments in there about Hatch that would bother him. But you know Dan. He'd probably say 'let it go.'" But I told him not to show it to Dan. I had neither desire nor need to solicit Quayle's comments—to borrow trouble with publication still years away. I had just wanted to test staff sentiment. "Hatch," incidentally was Senator Orrin Hatch of Utah, Chairman of the Full Labor Committee, someone with whom Subcommittee Chairman Quayle had had a rocky relationship. In the manuscript, I had quoted Quayle on Hatch: "Hatch is completely disorganized...I can't deal with him. I had to go around him...Hatch doesn't accomplish anything. What has he ever done?"

When I called Washington early on the morning on August 17th, a staff friend of mine answered. "I'm thinking of publishing some stuff about Dan," I said. "I'd like to talk to him about it." "All those decisions are out of our hands now," he said. "We'll talk around and get back to you." "I have a manuscript to show him," I said. "Send it down here and we'll get it to Dan," he said. "No," I said. The handlers had clearly taken command; I did not want my manuscript circulating out there somewhere among the handlers. He said they'd get back to me.

A couple of weeks later, Quayle's administrative assistant called to say that he had been shown the locked-up manuscript. When he said he liked the manuscript, I asked him what he thought Dan would say. "Well, there are a couple of comments he made about Hatch that might bother him, but you know Dan, he'd probably say 'go right ahead.'" When I asked him about getting the manuscript to Quayle, the aide explained how little input he was having into the campaign operation. But he also made it very clear that he believed the manuscript would help Dan and that he was eager for it to see the light of day. "Why should we stand in your way," he said, "We respect the integrity of your manuscript."

The net effect of this conversation was to permanently disabuse me of any idea that I might get the manuscript to Quayle in the middle of the campaign. I simply had no lines of communication I could trust. But I did have a couple of favorable "You know Dan" assessments from his two most trusted aides. And that reassured me for the duration.

Sure enough, when the contents of the book became known, it was his comments about Orrin Hatch that caused Quayle the most immediate difficulty. When he first saw them among some published excerpts in December, he had called Hatch to apologize. It was the first thing he mentioned when I brought him a copy of the book a couple of days later. He put his hands up to his head in mock horror. "When I saw that quote about Hatch, I said 'Oh my god, what's Fenno done to me?'" "I called Hatch," he went on, "I told him I was pretty frustrated at the time. I told him that I was really mad at his staff. Hatch said he knew that but he said 'and you were pretty mad at me, too.' And I told him, 'Yes, I was.'"

All this was said in good humor; he kicked me in the foot at one point and said "You rascal"; but clearly it was trouble he did not need. I told him my two "You know Dan" stories and I asked him, "If I had shown the book to you, what would you have done?" He fairly shouted the answer "Cut it out, cut it out." And he added, "If I did it again, I would say 'off the record, off the record.' I was very open with you, as you know."

Would I have taken it out had he asked me? I would have modified it; but I probably would not have taken it out entirely. For the relationship between committee chairman and subcommittee chairman is an important one in my study. I have learned, since, that the quotation gives authenticity and credibility to the book—as evidence that it was under my control, not his, that I was not afraid to embarrass him. The incident reminds us vividly, however, of something we already know, that personal relations among politicians are among the most sensitive of all real world subjects. And we need to be extremely careful when we deal with them.

In this particular case, Dan Quayle was not in a position to criticize. For it had become clear that he benefited by my book too much to complain about any part of it. And that was fine by me. Indeed I felt like the two of us had been to hell and back together. I had long since crossed the boundary in spirit; and I was pleased that the book was of help to him. The neutrality I had felt when I wrote the book was gone. I wanted him to do well as vice president.

When we met, I said to him "I know you better than almost anyone who is going to come through that door.... Do you mind if I give you a little advice?" He nodded for me to go ahead; and for 45 minutes I gave him some. That December meeting had sealed a relationship very much like the one with Conable in its effects. It put our relationship permanently on the far side of the boundary. Up to that point, I had done nothing to eliminate the possibility that I could continue to do research on Quayle as vice president. With my several interventions of that meeting, I had—to my mind—eliminated the option. In January, he called to say he had read the book. We talked about how it was doing. And I said to him, "All the attention that has fallen on you has fallen on me, too." "Welcome to the club," he said. I may never see Dan Quayle again. But, as a political scientist, I cannot do any research on him again either.

It remains an open question, whether my behavior in this case will affect my future access to politicians or the future access of other scholars. For I failed to follow the strictest possible interpretation of my own revised rule by removing the sensitive quotations from the manuscript. The fact that Quayle is in no position to criticize does not change the fact of his unhappiness with the Hatch material. And other politicians may look less favorably upon this kind of research because of it. Certainly, I hope not. I do not believe that I acted recklessly in this matter. It is not a kiss-and-tell book. But I worry about it. Problems of access—getting it, keeping it, and preserving it for others—are among the central worries in participant observation research. In the Conable case, I have evidence that my relationship with him helped later political scientists to gain special access to him and to do good research because of it. But the Senate case may be different, because the dilemmas attendant upon the practice of naming names will not likely go away. There will be many judgment calls. I can only hope that a desire to keep that research on the political science side of the boundary will lead to vigilance and self-restraint in the matter.

With the publication of the book, there was no doubt that my writing had put me—as I had always assumed it would—in politics. Immediately, the book began to be used by people in the political world for reasons and purposes of their own. Within a week, for example, *National Journal* and the *Washington Post* carried stories about it. The Table of Contents of *National Journal* carried the following reference to it: "Evaluating Quayle: A soon-to-be-published book on Senator Dan Quayle describes the vice president as neither a heroic figure nor an accomplished politician."[5] On page one of the *Post*, there appeared this index reference to it: "Quayle's Political Growth. Newly published book depicts Vice President Quayle as a sometimes profane politician who was bored in the House but came of age in the Senate."[6] The first article proved mostly negative, the second mostly positive. It was all out of my hands.

Except for interviews. Eventually, I did a lot of television, newspaper, and radio talk show interviews. And at this point the final temptation arose—the temptation to go beyond the evidence in the book to render other judgments on the vice president. With the main boundary line totally breached, I had to fall back to an interior line of professional defense. I was determined not to make any statements that could not be supported by the evidence of the book. To do so would only inject me further into the current political life of Dan Quayle and compromise the credibility of the book as political science. While I still wanted him to do well, I did not want to get publicly involved. The temptations were almost always to make favorable predictions concerning his performance as vice president—to become, in effect, his press agent. I tried hard to abstain from such judgments, to hold to the response that "I can only tell you what I saw." "I have no idea how he'll do as vice president," I would say, adding only that "one finding from my book was that he grew a great deal in the Senate. And if he grew once, one could imagine that he can grow some more." I cannot render an informed verdict on my success in drawing the line there, but I have tried. The Quayle hunt of the campaign has now turned into the Quayle watch of the vice presidency. The hunters have become watchers; and I have, so far, been as absent from the second group as from the first. This final interventionist wrinkle is another reminder that boundary maintenance problems are as omnipresent after the research is done as they are while it is being done—in this case, even after it has been published.

The Quayle experience demonstrates, above all, that we learn by experience in doing participant observation. It demonstrates, further, that we cannot anticipate all the experiences we will confront as we ply our trade back and forth across the boundary between political science and the political world. The ambiguities, the varieties, and the tentativeness of our experience make hard and fast research canons difficult to come by and

---

[5]"Evaluating Quayle," *National Journal*, December 10, 1988, p. 3109; Dom Bonafede, "An Account of Quayle's Charmed Life," *National Journal*, December 10, 1988, pp. 3134-3135.

[6]"Quayle's Political Growth," *Washington Post*, December 14, 1988, p. 1; David Broder, "Book Traces Quayle's Evolution from Bored, Confident Congressman," *Washington Post*, December 14, 1988, p. A23.

difficult to hold to. But there is a set of worries that applies to all contexts with all politicians, and must be kept constantly in mind.

One worry, which achieved special prominence in the Quayle case, is the existence of an emotional relationship between researcher and politician, between observer and observed. The Quayle case threw this problem into such stark relief that it caused me to exhume the Barber Conable case—previously buried in a couple of sentences as an exception. Given the similarities with the Quayle case, it now seems less of an exception than it once did. The two cases suggest strongly that more emotion than we might wish to acknowledge lies—unprovoked and untested—just below the surface of our relations with politicians and will be brought into the open under certain circumstances.

As of 5:55 p.m., August 16th, my relationship with Senator Dan Quayle was no different from the routine, low key, fairly antiseptic relationships I had established and maintained with dozens of other politicians during my career. Yet within minutes, I was put on an emotional roller coaster that affected a succession of subsequent research-related choices.

There are a lot of reasons why we who spend so much of our working lives with politicians, should develop sympathetic ties to them. Politics is a full-time job for its practitioners. And it is more of a full-time job for participant observers than it is for most other political scientists. It actively engages us physically and psychologically more regularly than most research modes. For those who might doubt this, a few months eating, sleeping, and drinking your research in the hyper-political Washington environment or in the frenetic, "us and them" environment of a campaign will provide proof enough. To the degree that politics is a full-time preoccupation for us, it captures and calls upon our emotions as much as our ideas. And therein lies both its pleasures and its pitfalls. When you are around one group of people a lot cultivating trusting relationships with them, you cannot help gaining sympathy for them, getting to like them and feeling some gratitude for opening up to you in a situation where they have so little to gain.

Our work inevitably places us for extended periods of time in the company of sympathetic figures and in the middle of consequential activity. For the individual researcher, however, professional credibility must remain the most salient value. This value can only be kept uppermost in our thinking if we assume some separation between the world of political science and the world of politics and if we assume some kind of boundary between them. Absent any restraining notions of professional integrity, all sorts of invitations, seductions, and temptations exist to roam all over the political landscape—now researching, now participating, now being an amateur at politics, now being an amateur at research, without any active concern for which was which or who we are. Participant observation is not a path to politics; it is a path to political science. There is a big need in our business for more people to study politicians, not to become politicians.

Our business is to generalize about politics and, thereby, to contribute to the common enterprise of the political science community. We live within that community. Our standards are generated there. Our credibility is tested there. Our contribution gets evaluated there. We exchange research and build understanding there. It is for our colleagues as well as for ourselves that we need to locate our work solidly and unmistakably within the political science community. And use that location to think carefully, with them, about our research.

We shall have to set some research standards even though experience may cause us to alter them. We shall have to fix some research boundaries even though experience may cause us to breach them. The rule in such matters is to set standards that will command respect in the political science community and give ground grudgingly. If the Quayle experience is any guide, however, we will have to give ground from time to time. Implicitly, I believe, the standards set in the *Home Style* Appendix are standards to shoot for; but the Quayle experience has forced me to make that sense of approximation more explicit. There will never be, alas, a final appendix. So, we shall need to keep on observing, keep on learning, keep on worrying, keep on publishing, and keep on writing appendices—at every stage of the process. With the proviso that we do all this, openly and self-consciously, as part of the political science community. For it is only within that community, I believe, that we can put our experience to its most constructive purpose.

2

Political Scientists and Journalists:
The Dan Quayle Experience

On Tuesday, August 16th, when Senator Dan Quayle was picked by George Bush to be his vice-presidential running mate, I had a finished 253 page manuscript on Dan Quayle sitting in my desk drawer. Except for this manuscript, Quayle was an unexamined—and hence unknown—public figure. I was, therefore, put in the strange position of watching the nation's journalists begin to gather information and form judgments on someone about whom I had finished gathering information and forming judgments a year earlier. The situation presented a kind of natural experiment. Would they see what I had seen? Would their conclusions match mine? If so, why? If not, why not?

My decision to abstain totally from the campaign preserved the experiment for the duration. From their standpoint, the journalists would proceed with their task in total isolation from anything I had said or done. From my standpoint, their performance would provide a unique check on my performance as a participant observer.

Perspective

It was almost no time at all before the overall dimensions of the comparison began to appear. As I watched the journalists develop and express their views, they seemed to be taking quite a different shape from my own. And the more their views came into focus, the greater the difference seemed to become. In my settled view, Dan Quayle was a senator who had both impressive electoral victories and a significant legislative accomplishment to his credit, who had grown measurably during his six years in the Senate, and who, on that record, displayed both political abilities and political promise. According to the developing journalistic view, Quayle was a lightweight, a person without sufficient intellect or maturity, experience or accomplishment, or depth of character to be vice president.

While these two views were not technically incompatible, since we were judging him at two different points in time and in terms of two different offices, the thrust of the two judgments *was* different—*very different*. Too different, it seemed to me, to be explained solely by reference to the effects of timing and office. And different enough to encourage some attention to the observers themselves—to political scientists and journalists.

Political scientists who study politicians at close range have a lot in common with journalists. We do the same thing. We watch and we talk and we do it in the same place—that is, in the real political world. Journalists are people with whom we regularly come in contact as we go about our research; their reporting is invaluable to us; and they are people whose judgments we value when our work is finished. But they live in the political world, and we only work there. Or so the notions of separateness and boundaries prescribe for us. Indeed, by living on the far side of the boundary, journalists help to locate it for us.

One of the constant interventionist temptations for those of us who cross over into the political world to do our research is to join the journalists, to become pundits and commentators on the passing political scene. As we cope with that temptation, we are forced to think about disciplinary boundaries that separate political science from political journalism.

The affinities between us, as I say, are strong. But when that has been acknowledged, it remains true that political science is *not* journalism. And it is one of the crucial tasks of boundary maintenance that political scientists maintain that distinction. The goals, the standards, the audience, the work environments and the work habits of the two occupations, the two professions are different. And those differences, in turn, help to account for differences in our work product.

The analysis I wish to undertake depends heavily on a "journalism watch" that I began on the evening of Bush's announcement, which I kept up with some care for the next couple of weeks, and which I kept up sporadically thereafter, until inauguration day. This journalism watch was highly impressionistic; and it was totally biased by my own unique angle of vision. My special bias was an overriding concern for the journalists' treatment of Quayle's performance in the passage of the Job Training Partnership Act. That legislative story was the centerpiece of my book; it constituted the main body of evidence on which I had based my picture of the Senator.

Early on, as I have said, I believed that if I did not publish quickly, the journalistic community would soon dig into everything I had dug into and write my story before I did. I waited with special anticipation, therefore, for them to undertake that investigative effort. Surprisingly, as it turned out, they never did. So the question "Why didn't they" gave an extra push to my own special curiosity and my own special perspective.

In what follows, I shall speak often of "the journalistic community." I know that in order to do any kind of serious analysis I should make distinctions at least between the television and the print media if not within each medium. I shall try to indicate which of the major media sources I am talking about, but my generalizations will apply to all of them collectively—that is, to "the journalistic community." While there are exceptions, I believe that at the level of generalization I shall be operating, TV and print media behaved similarly and can be lumped together. And I shall do my best to support that assumption.

Certain occupational conditions affect all political journalists—their goals, their standards, their audience, their work environment, their work habits. Those are the ones I shall emphasize. Political journalists believe that the free press plays an important part in the democratic process by informing the public, thereby linking the governed to the government and the electorate to their politicians. So they believe that they help the public to understand and to judge both their government and their politicians. But there is a built-in, occupational desire to keep a distance from government and politicians—a product of their own efforts at boundary maintenance. This effort calls for and results in a critical, suspicious stance toward politicians and a fear of being manipulated by them, which has produced, in Meg Greenfield's words, "a super suspicious, show me press."[1] Journalists also work under conditions of great pressure—time pressure and competitive pressure. They must produce the news according to an inexorable timetable, with one eye on what and how others in their business are doing. Their time horizons are short. The competition to attract and keep an audience pressures them to produce "the story," even though it may not be fully developed or fully documented. They deal, of course, in information, which they may have to take on the run, from a variety of sources, catch as catch can. They will try to increase the availability and reliability of information by cultivating regular sources.

---

[1]Meg Greenfield, "The Press and Dan Quayle," *Newsweek*, September 5, 1988.

These sources can be helpful, but they can also imprison the journalist and narrow his or her perspective.

Competitive pressures can create incentives for a journalist to produce breaking news or an investigative scoop that beats the competition and frames "the story." But the constant monitoring of one's competitors can also produce a homogeneity of outlook, generate a premature consensus on what "the story" is, and reduce incentives to investigate further. When hundreds of journalists are thrown together, as at convention time, to report on the same events, the incentives to satisfy editors by joining and then following one's colleagues are strong. In his critique of 1988 campaign reporting, Marvin Kalb accused the press of laziness, of coalescing in a pack and "neglecting the virtues of old fashioned legwork."[2]

In the business of getting and reporting the news, journalists have increasingly moved away from a "just the facts" approach to a more interpretive form of reporting. This form requires some underlying story line or theme to sustain the story, to tell the audience what it all means. Given their need to hold the attention of the audience, they tend to present their story line in simplified and dramatic form. One way to build drama is to concentrate on the main characters, to emphasize patterns of personality, and to build themes around the characteristics and activities of individual politicians. Given their own occupational suspicion of politicians, given the pressures under which they operate, and given audience receptivity to politician-centered drama, it is not surprising that their thematic presentations of the news often tend toward the short term, the personal, and the negative instead of the long term, the institutional, and the positive. Once these themes are established, the incentives to satisfice and hang onto them are strong.

This is a wholly amateurish stab at describing some of the conditions of the journalistic occupation. But I make the stab because I believe some awareness of their working conditions will be helpful in explaining the press's treatment of Dan Quayle. I shall present that treatment, however, in terms of *process*—to try and understand journalistic behavior by focussing on the sequence of events, reactions, information flows, and interpretations that affected the journalists and resulted in their acceptance and presentation of a certain portrait of Dan Quayle.

The period of maximum journalistic attention to Quayle occurred during the first ten-day to two-week period following his selection. It is my overall view that a journalistic consensus crystallized quickly and solidly during this period and remained unchanged throughout the campaign.

---

[2]Marvin Kalb, "How the Media Distorted the Race," *Atlanta Journal-Atlanta Constitution*, November 1988.

Reactions

When it came, on Tuesday the 16th, Bush's announcement was a surprise—in two senses. Bush had kept his thinking a secret from everyone; Quayle had never been considered the favorite in media speculation. The journalistic community, therefore, had very little time or incentive to prepare in any depth for the Quayle selection.

Credit for first mentioning his name was given to the *New York Times* for an article on Saturday the 13th—only three days before the announcement. It reported that "surprisingly strong support has emerged" for Quayle; but it still rated him no more than "a dark horse conservative option."[3] *Newsweek's* Monday edition assessed the chances of nine vice-presidential possibilities; but Quayle was not one of them. Articles in the *New York Times*, the *Wall Street Journal* and the *Washington Post* on the day of the selection listed Quayle in an array of four to six possibilities. When the announcement came late that afternoon, the journalistic community had to work under intense time pressure and intense competitive pressure to gather information and make judgments on someone they knew virtually nothing about.

Their situation was reflected in their own commentary that evening. "He was at the bottom of everybody's list.... [It's a] shock," said John Chancellor.[4] "A thunderbolt has hit the superdome, and the lightning has yet to subside," said Dan Rather to open his convention coverage. "Want to see what he looks like?" Peter Jennings asked his audience. CNN's Bernard Shaw called him "J. Dan Quayle." Jim Lehrer began his interviews on the subject saying, "Robin gave me a profile of Dan Quayle that I read before I came in a little while ago, and the article said...." Ted Koppel began his program, "We know his name, but we do not know who he is." The Bush campaign had hurriedly xeroxed copies of the *Almanac of American Politics* that afternoon. As *Newsweek* later reported, "TV pundits spoke knowledgeably about him—in sentences lifted almost intact from the *Almanac*...."[5] They were all scrambling to catch up and to catch on. They were searching for themes to sustain their commentary. And they made their own surprise and their own lack of information their first—and their most perishable—theme.

But along with this theme they voiced another less perishable one—that Dan Quayle was not just unknown but also as they put it "untested" or "untested in a national campaign." By which they meant untested *by them*.

---

[3]Gerald Boyd, "Bush Prunes Running-Mate List; One is A Dark Horse from Indiana," *New York Times*, August 13, 1988.

[4]All television commentary cited in the article, except where printed texts can be cited, came from tape recordings.

[5]"Conventional-Wisdom Watch," *Newsweek*, August 29, 1988.

They commonly referred to the selection as "a risk" or "a risky choice" for Bush because Quayle had not yet "felt the heat" or endured the ordeal by fire—that is, the heat and fire of the press—during a high-profile campaign. In the life of every national public figure there comes a time of testing—be it in Washington or on the campaign trail—during which the national press takes a look and renders a judgment, which, if favorable, bestows a threshold judgment of legitimacy on that person. It is not approval or even sympathy; it is a judgment about qualification for office and credibility in performance. Clearly, Dan Quayle's testing time was at hand.

The earliest presentation gave no cause for optimism. For it seemed to me that the journalists much preferred a vice-presidential candidate who had already been tested and certified by them. In that respect, they seemed disappointed, if not unhappy, with Bush's choice. Mark Shields expressed it best on the MacNeil/Lehrer show that night. "Today," he began,

> the jury is more than out.... It is not a strong choice.... Let me tell you what the Bush people said, and this was—it was all over this city—the one thing we want to be sure of is we're going to have somebody who the press is going to have respect for. That was their litmus test. And certainly in the case of Bob Dole and I think Jack Kemp...there was a sense of gravitas, of Alan Simpson, most definitely. That was the case of Pete Domenici; that was not of Dan Quayle. Now maybe that's unfair on the press's part. That's something they're going to have to overcome.... Can one think right now of Dan Quayle as Assistant President? I would say that most people who have covered politics could not.[6]

The idea seemed to be that the press, too, had a stake in the selection; that George Bush, by selecting someone they had not taken seriously, had let them down. It was as if his judgment was a reflection on their judgment. Had the choice been Bob Dole or Jack Kemp, one can imagine that Shields would have reacted very differently. He would have expressed community satisfaction in the sense that the person chosen would have been known to them, tested by them, and pronounced legitimate by them. And he would have bellied up to the bar immediately and comfortably with the new candidate.

Dan Quayle was not the media's choice. He had arrived on the scene untested, without journalistic certification, and worse, without journalistic neutrality. David Gergen, on the same program as Shields, put it this way. "I think it's not going to play [as] well among the press. There is a feeling among those in the press that he's too young for the job, that he

---

[6]Transcript, MacNeil/Lehrer Newshour, August 16, 1988.

may be inexperienced. You hear the word 'light' frequently about him. I think he's going to have to prove himself with the press."[7] Whether the press would overcome or suspend their criticism of the choice long enough to give Dan Quayle a fair hearing, was a very open question. In my view, the untested stranger in their midst seemed disadvantaged from the outset.

Indeed, such judgments about Quayle's qualifications as had begun to circulate in the day or two before he was chosen were negative; and the journalistic community had prematurely dismissed Quayle's chances largely on that very basis. On Sunday, a preselection article about Quayle in the *Boston Globe* repeatedly cited Republican sources as criticizing and dismissing the Indiana senator. "GOP sources point out that his lack of accomplishment in 12 years in Congress makes his selection unlikely," it said. And, "Republican sources in the Senate...expressed incredulity over the possibility.... Several sources described him as a lightweight."[8] Monday's long *Los Angeles Times* windup VP story mentioned Quayle at the very end and closed with the comment that "Republican aides...scoffed at rumors the choice might be Quayle."[9]

We can assume that anyone else who had inquired between Saturday and Tuesday could have turned up that same judgment—that Dan Quayle was not to be taken seriously. That was exactly the judgment, for example, of Washington analyst Norman Ornstein, a frequent source of media opinion. Pronouncing himself "stunned" by the choice, he said immediately afterwards, "I didn't think Quayle was a serious possibility. And I don't think he should have been a serious possibility."[10] When Quayle was chosen, the journalistic community was primed, if anything, to prove themselves right and Bush wrong.

Within hours of Bush's announcement, this negative judgment was being widely dispensed by the press. "Dan Quayle was the only person on the list who did not intellectually intimidate George Bush" said Mark Shields.[11] "Is he a lightweight?" Leslie Stahl asked politicians on the convention floor. "The knock on Senator Quayle as you hear it buzzing around this hall,..." reported Brit Hume, "has been that he's a lightweight." Judd Rose concluded, "Already there's some talk that Bush has picked, to be blunt, a lightweight." "No one yet has described him as a heavyweight,"

---

[7]*Ibid.*

[8]Curtis Wilkie, "Indiana Senator Stuns Some By Appearing on Bush List," *Boston Globe*, August 14, 1988.

[9]Jack Nelson, "Bush Holds Final Session on Ticket: Simpson Bows Out as Running Mate Contender, Gives Support to Senator Dole," *Los Angeles Times*, August 15, 1988.

[10]Robert Shogan, "Bush Choice Means He'll Carry the Burden Alone: Quayle's Help to Ticket Questioned," *Los Angeles Times*, August 17, 1988.

[11]Transcript, MacNeil/Lehrer Newshour, August 16, 1988.

Ted Koppel suggested to a Republican guest on *Nightline*. "Would you like to be the first?" By the end of the first evening, this judgment—that Dan Quayle was an unaccomplished lightweight—had been implanted in, if not accepted by, the journalistic community.

By the end of the second evening it seemed solidly established as a major theme of media commentary. On the MacNeil/Lehrer Newshour, David Gergen concluded that "the coverage on television last night and this morning has been pretty negative. There have been accusations of a stature gap, that he doesn't have the experience or weight.... I think it's hard to find a journalist in this town, a serious journalist, who is high on Dan Quayle.... They question whether he's qualified...I do think he starts with a handicap."[12] And Mark Shields added that "[Press reaction] is going to be influential...it's a serious problem, because first impressions do not go away."[13] A complementary theme adding spicey suspense to this one was, of course, that George Bush might have damaged himself seriously if not irretrievably by his choice.

As I listened to these various renderings of a negative journalistic judgment, I reflected on the manuscript in my desk drawer. It credited Dan Quayle with a substantial, subcommittee-to-conference committee legislative accomplishment—with a display of responsible leadership, good political instincts, bipartisan coalition building skills, and perseverance in the face of unremitting opposition from his own administration. The Job Training Partnership Act (JTPA), of which he was indisputably the leading architect, sponsor, strategist, and political shepherd, was, arguably, the most important new piece of social legislation passed by the 97th Congress. Even more important, it was the best example, if not the only example, of what Dan Quayle would do when the Senate or anyone else gave him the responsibility to do a job. And my manuscript had argued that, in 1986, the voters of Indiana had recognized and rewarded him for precisely that legislative performance.[14] George Bush had extolled that same performance when he made the announcement on Tuesday. And it was there in the record for all to see.

The only mention of JTPA I had seen in the few days before the selection appeared in the *Globe* article cited earlier—in the following paragraph.

> Skeptics also say Quayle's congressional record does little to merit consideration. His most memorable performance in nearly eight years in the Senate was a compromise jobs training act he wrote with Senator Edward M. Kennedy.

---

[12]*Ibid.*, August 17, 1988.
[13]*Ibid.*
[14]See Richard F. Fenno, Jr., *The Making of a Senator: Dan Quayle*, Washington: CQ Press, 1988.

> A Democrat, who served with Quayle, remembered the
> Hoosier yesterday as a pleasant, affable, nice looking fellow
> whose record in the House was a complete cipher. He is
> not a heavyweight.[15]

It was a mention. And it *was* "his most memorable performance." But
the mention was crafted and presented so as to draw a minimal amount
of attention, convey a minimal amount of positive force, and pose a
minimal threat to the main theme of the unaccomplished lightweight.

This preselection article became a blueprint for what was to follow
during the first couple of days after the announcement. JTPA would
occasionally get mentioned, but never in any depth. Often his House
career would be given equal billing with his Senate career; sometimes,
analysis would stop altogether at the end of his House career. JTPA did
not draw the early attention of a single journalist among all that I heard
or taped or read. Yet, it seemed to me, it needed to command serious,
if not sustained, journalistic attention if the unaccomplished lightweight
theme were to be counteracted or altered.

The first evening, each of the networks called upon their regular
Capitol Hill and/or Washington correspondents to profile Dan Quayle.
A priori one would have thought that these people on the political beat
would know about, and would give some attention to, Dan Quayle's major
legislative accomplishment. And journalists who had not worked close-
in to Congress would then take information and judgmental cues from
their more knowledgeable colleagues. But neither Brit Hume nor Sam
Donaldson of ABC, neither Phil Jones or Leslie Stahl of CBS, and neither
John Dancy nor Chris Wallace of NBC mentioned JTPA. And not one of
them even mentioned that Dan Quayle was a member of the Labor and
Human Resources Committee. Several of them, however, mentioned his
service on Armed Services and Budget. The only brush with JTPA all
evening was Dancy's mention that Quayle pushed the private sector to get
involved in job training programs—to buttress Dancy's theme that the
senator was a conservative. If there was to be a positive JTPA story line
presented to the journalistic community, it was not going to come from
the one group of colleagues in the best position to know something about
it.

I recalled, from my manuscript, that the press in general had not been
interested in the legislation when it had passed and that Quayle had been
conspicuously uninterested in generating publicity or taking credit for his
accomplishment. And I wondered whether his marked inattention to the
care and feeding of the Washington press might be coming back to hurt
him. Again, it was as if the community was simply expressing a long

---

[15]Curtis Wilkie, "Indiana Senator Stuns Some...."

standing judgment that the senator from Indiana was not to be taken seriously. It was a judgment made, however, without any effort to incorporate the most relevant information.

In the course of press interviews with Republican politicians at the convention, JTPA did get mentioned fairly often and always positively by the interviewees. The Bush people had been primed to mention it, and they did so. But in a perfunctory, obligatory manner, without informational backup or sustained enthusiasm. So another potential source of positive information failed to materialize. The Bush people had not had time to put together a story line about Quayle—and this left the Republican presentation to the media devoid of any sustaining theme. Besides which, there was an undercurrent of dissent and disappointment leaking out of the Bush camp itself—perhaps from some of the same "sources" that had fed the preselection stories. Bill Plante commented the first night, for example, that "Some political pros inside the Bush campaign [are] stunned.... They did not expect it, they never dreamed it would happen...they thought the guy is inexperienced, young, he's a lightweight." Reporters, who feed on conflict, seemed to have no difficulty digging up negative comments about Quayle from disgruntled Republicans. Some of his Senate colleagues who had been passed over by Bush were notably unhelpful.

To my knowledge, there were only two instances when JTPA drew extended mention from interviewees that first evening. When Brit Hume posed the lightweight question directly to Senator Orrin Hatch, Chairman of the Labor Committee, he got this response:

> I don't think you can say the author of the Job Training
> Partnership Act—which is probably the most important
> piece of legislation which has come out of this
> Administration—is a lightweight. I know. I worked very
> closely with Dan to bring that piece of legislation forth....

It was the most positive, most informed, most ringing mention of Quayle's leadership on JTPA that I heard or read for at least a week. But neither Hume on the floor nor Peter Jennings and David Brinkley in the ABC anchor booth followed up or mentioned it again. It was dead on delivery.

The second instance occurred on *Nightline*, when Ted Koppel asked former Indiana Democratic Congressman Floyd Fithian whether "anything happened" in the Senate to cause Fithian to "reassess" his opinion that Quayle "left no tracks in the House as far as accomplishment is concerned...." Fithian answered,

> There was one significant achievement which ought not to
> be overlooked, and that is his joining Senator Kennedy on
> the JTPA, a major piece of legislation. It was a surprise

36

to those of us who knew Dan that he would be on that kind of a bill.

Again, it was a mention, but one which described Quayle's "significant achievement" as "joining" and "being on" the bill. And even that was clearly an exception not diagnostic. Just to make certain he was understood, Fithian added that it was "frightening" to think of Dan Quayle as vice president. Koppel did not pick up on JTPA. Nor did he, later in the program, when an Indiana reporter cited that law as "a major piece of social legislation in the Reagan administration" for which Quayle would be remembered. This total lack of early interest in JTPA within the journalistic community was striking.

The following day, at their joint press conference, George Bush had bracketed the proceedings with specific praise for Quayle's JTPA performance—opening and closing the conference on that theme. Yet not a single question was asked about it. That evening, the MacNeil/Lehrer segment on Dan Quayle opened with Bush's closing comment at the press conference: "His leadership in this Job Training Partnership Act, really something sensational." But in the follow-up discussion, not one of the five well-known journalists assembled for their analysis of the Quayle selection paid any attention to that accolade. Instead, each one delivered broadly negative assessments of Quayle's abilities.[16] And later that evening, when Quayle himself—in an interview with Tom Brokaw—opened by citing his leadership on job training legislation, and his bipartisan approach with Ted Kennedy, Brokaw moved to other subjects. And it was not mentioned for the rest of the evening.

Another potential source of positive information also failed to develop. From the first evening, and to the end of the campaign, people informed about Dan Quayle's work on defense matters spoke out enthusiastically and in detail about his competence in that policy field—Jeane Kirkpatrick, Henry Kissinger, Richard Perle, Kenneth Adelman, Donald Rumsfield.[17] But not one leading expert in the job training field spoke up to praise Quayle's record. For they were all liberal and labor-oriented Democrats, for whom Quayle's bill had been too much of a compromise to deserve enthusiastic praise. So the issue-network people who applauded his gutsy fight against the Reagan administration were no help to him when he

---

[16]Transcript, MacNeil/Lehrer Newshour, August 17, 1988. The journalists were: R. W. Apple, *New York Times*; Howard Fineman, *Newsweek*; David Gergen, *U.S. News and World Report*; Jon Margolis, *Chicago Tribune*; Mark Shields, *Washington Post.*

[17]Jeane Kirkpatrick on August 16th on CBS; Kenneth Adelman, "Dan Quayle: Not Just Another Pretty Face," *Wall Street Journal*, August 25, 1988; Richard Perle, "Dan Quayle's Got the Right Stuff," *New York Times*, October 25, 1988; Donald Rumsfield, "Quayle Meets the Test," *Chicago Tribune*, November 3, 1988.

needed them in the partisan political world beyond the Senate. Such are the hazards of political independence.

These hazards were compounded by a tendency among media commentators to view Quayle's job training efforts through the eyes of organized labor. And that helped to give even their brief mentions a negative spin. "He irritated the White House by sponsoring a $3 billion a year jobs training act for the unemployed, yet he is no friend of labor," CBS's veteran congressional correspondent broadcast on August 17th. On the same day, a top political reporter of the *Los Angeles Times* wrote, "And although he was involved in promoting a job training program with Senator Edward Kennedy, Quayle opposed to the bitter end the controversial plant closing notification bill that Reagan himself allowed to become law because of its symbolic importance to labor."[18] These minimal, backhanded references to JTPA would be all it ever got from either of the two reporters involved.

The journalistic community seemed not to be attracted to the idea that there might be something out there worth talking about. There was an endless amount of questioning about why Bush chose Quayle, but not a single suggestion that George Bush's praise of Dan Quayle's JTPA performance might conceivably suggest a partial answer to that question. Despite numerous stimuli, not once in two days, on *any* of the three major networks, did *any* journalist follow up on *any* mention of the JTPA by *any* interviewee. Its importance seemed to have been discounted before it was ever understood.

Themes

Wednesday's and Thursday's newspapers, by contrast, usually mentioned JTPA—a distinct improvement over television, but not a significant one. The print media has a larger newshole and can be expected to include a broader range of information. They also had more time and reportorial resources to commit to the preparation of their reaction. So they could be expected to at least mention Quayle's major senatorial accomplishment. Which they did. But mentioning did not mean emphasizing. Whatever their preliminary research, it did not lead any of them to give more than minimal coverage to JTPA. And they remained, for example, as interested in Ted Kennedy's presence as in Dan Quayle's leadership.

If we consider the five earliest profiles of Dan Quayle, published on Wednesday or Thursday in the *Washington Post, New York Times, Wall Street Journal, Los Angeles Times,* and *Boston Globe*, they consumed a total of 219 column inches. Of that total, only 7½" or 3 percent of the

---

[18]Phil Jones of CBS; Robert Shogan "Bush Choice Means He'll Carry the Burden Alone...."

coverage was devoted to JTPA—or about one inch of coverage for every 30 column inches.

Equally indicative of newspaper interest and attention was the actual treatment of JTPA in the profiles. The most complimentary of the five was in the *Washington Post*. While it was a distinctly minor theme of the profile, JTPA was treated as a positive accomplishment. It commanded an unusual 10 percent of the profile; and the *Post*, alone of the five, mentioned JTPA in the top half of its profile. "Quayle," it said, "made a solid, if not widely recognized mark as the prime mover behind the 1982 Job Training Partnership Act, working with such Democrats as Edward Kennedy." It added that the "effectiveness" of JTPA "has since been hailed by both parties." Later, in the final two paragraphs of the profile, it said, "he shepherded new job training legislation through Congress." And it named his subcommittee. But the last word was given to Democrat Paul Simon who said, "It's an area where he [got] away from being just a Republican ideologue."[19] The total impression left is that JTPA was an exception, rather than a base from which to predict future behavior. But that profile was the best JTPA look he got. And it would be, so far as I know, the best journalistic look he would ever get, excepting only one column, written interestingly enough by someone who had watched his Senate performance very carefully—Michael Barone, the editor of the *Almanac of American Politics*.[20]

The four other early profiles gave JTPA even more of an exceptionalist treatment. The *New York Times* profile, 50 inches long, contained not a single mention or hint of it. "In the Senate," it generalized, "he has established himself as a diligent legislator willing to tackle complex military issues and faithfully pulling his weight for conservative causes."[21] The *Wall Street Journal's* only mention came in the following paragraph: "Mr. Quayle has been a faithful conservative and a hard-liner on defense issues. But he has shown flexibility by reaching out to liberals such as Senator Edward Kennedy on job training issues important to workers in blue collar Indiana."[22] The *Los Angeles Times* profile described Quayle as "an energetic, affable conservative who

---

[19]Helen Dewar and David Broder, "A Reagan Conservative: Hoosier Scrappy, Rich, Telegenic," *Washington Post*, August 17, 1988.

[20]Michael Barone, "A New Breed of Baby Boomer," *Washington Post*, August 18, 1988. See also his later article, Michael Barone, "Quayle: Here's the Rest of Him," *Washington Post*, September 30, 1988. Another late but balanced treatment is: Richard Cohen, "Second Fiddles," *National Journal*, October 29, 1988.

[21]Susan Rasky, "Baby Boomer with Right Credentials," *New York Times*, August 17, 1988.

[22]James Perry, "Bush Discloses He Wants Senator Quayle, A Young Conservative, As Running Mate," *Wall Street Journal*, August 17, 1988.

specializes in defense and health matters." But near the end of the profile it said, "As a member of the Senate Labor Committee, Quayle helped to devise and enact a successor program to the controversial Comprehensive Employment and Training Act. In so doing he worked closely with liberal Democratic Senator Edward Kennedy."[23] The *Boston Globe* generalized that "He has served in Congress for 12 years, but has won little recognition." Its paragraph on JTPA, once again positioned late in the profile, says that he "joined with Senator Edward Kennedy to develop a compromise job training bill." And it added that "A source from Kennedy's office recalled yesterday that Quayle had resisted pressure from the administration and pushed the bill to passage. It is one of the few initiatives that Quayle has undertaken in Congress that his colleagues remember."[24]

There is very little sense of Quayle's special responsibility or his leadership in all of this and certainly no notion that JTPA was a substantial enough achievement to be diagnostic for an assessment of Quayle's past much less his future. It is relegated to a perfunctory mention and left totally unconnected to any overall judgments on his Senate record. There is, in short, nothing here to call any special attention to it. After two days, therefore, the diagnostic importance of JTPA, in the judgment of the journalistic community—TV and print— ranged from zero to minimal. And their judgment on Dan Quayle the politician was overwhelmingly unfavorable.

Perhaps the press people believed they were being manipulated and perhaps that fear triumphed over their curiosity. The journalists did spend much of the 1988 campaign complaining that they were being manipulated by the candidates and their campaigners. But the Quayle case was, perhaps, the one instance in which they were not being manipulated. Their lack of follow-up was completely a matter of choice. They chose to neglect and/or downplay the single most outstanding performance of his public life. And because of that choice, their unaccomplished lightweight image stood unchallenged and unmodified. And it would be repeated to the end of the campaign.

Besides the unaccomplished lightweight theme, two other themes dominated media coverage in the first couple of days: that he was very conservative and very rich. His conservatism was a matter of record; and it was doubtless one of the important criteria in Bush's calculation. It was no surprise, then, to find all the television commentators emphasizing it throughout the first evening. They spoke of his "solid conservative

---

[23]Sara Fritz, "Quayle 1st Baby Boom Member for No. 2 Spot," *Los Angeles Times*, August 17, 1988.

[24]Curtis Wilkie, "Career in Congress Has Won Little Notice," *Boston Globe*, August 17, 1988.

credentials on all the major issues" or his "increasingly strong voice in conservative Republican ranks" or "an undisputed conservative...a little Ronald Reagan no doubt about that." Calling him "strong with the right in the Republican party," Dan Rather said that "People to the right of George Bush [are] overjoyed." "The conservatives in the Republican party," said David Brinkley, "are so happy they don't quite know what to do. They are delighted with Dan Quayle; he is their kind of person and has a pretty good record in the Senate."

That theme remained strong throughout the campaign. And it was, overall, accurate. But to the degree that it hardened into a stereotype—of the "Republican ideologue" to use Paul Simon's description—the conservatism theme militated against any close look at the job training bill. For that bill was far less an example of Quayle's conservatism than of his political moderation and his legislative pragmatism in the face of a problem for which he had assumed primary responsibility. To put it another way, anyone who believed that Dan Quayle's conservatism was "all of him," would have no incentive to look at his performance on JTPA. It was, therefore, the second journalistic theme to put Dan Quayle at an initial disadvantage in his quest for a fair hearing and for threshold legitimacy.

The third theme that emerged from the very first commentaries was not much help to Quayle either—that is, his family wealth. The extent to which the media fastened onto this idea *was* a surprise—to me at least—because I had never been particularly conscious of it. On Tuesday's NBC evening news, Tom Brokaw's very first description was "a wealthy young conservative." He introduced John Dancy's profile as "a look at the personal side of this millionaire senator." And in the first sentence of his evening convention coverage he introduced "the gold plated Republican party ticket, George Herbert Walker Bush and J. Danforth Quayle." Leslie Stahl began her Quayle profile: "Heir to an Indiana publishing empire, Quayle has the same silver spoon image as George Bush, although Quayle is many times wealthier...worth as much as 200 million." On CNN, Robert Novak said of Quayle, "He's one of the richest young men in America. He's worth 650 million." Later in the evening, Diane Sawyer followed suit by upping CBS' estimate from 200 to 650 million. Floor correspondents pushed the "rich young man" theme in their interviews. "They are both very rich men. Isn't that going to be a problem?" Chris Wallace asked one interviewee. And Dan Rather asked another, "Dan Quayle will inherit an immense fortune. He's already a very wealthy man. How does this help Bush?" Dennis Murphy began his extended Wednesday profile with, "Quayle, son of a wealthy newspaper publishing family—fortune estimated in the hundreds of millions of dollars..." etc.

Wednesday's print stories referred to him as "scion of a rich and powerful family" or "scion to a wealthy publishing family whose fortune makes him far richer than the well-to-do Bush" and "scion of an Indiana family that made its fortune in a chain of right wing newspapers."[25] After two days of media scrutiny, the idea of Dan Quayle's family wealth had become a factual staple of his profile. By itself, it might have had a short half life—especially since it was a factual exaggeration. But it was there to exemplify his privileged background and to be extended to include his privileged access to power when, on the third day, the National Guard controversy erupted.

Part of my story thus far is that the suddenness of Bush's announcement left the Republicans without sufficient time to produce any thematic justification, that a number of other potential media sources of information failed to produce supportive information, and that in this low information context the early media picture of Dan Quayle—as an untested, wealthy, conservative lightweight—took root.

There was, however, one group that worked actively to feed this negative image—the Democrats. The Democrats pressed their case with the media immediately after the announcement on Tuesday. Indeed, they appear to have been better prepared than the Republicans with a story line on the nominee. And the TV reporters taking information, we would guess, from wherever they could get it were clearly utilizing the Democratic materials and their Democratic sources.

Tom Brokaw commented that the Democrats had put out some "pretty good" material. "They've already got out 2½ pages on Quayle and deficits and privilege," he said. Peter Jennings said that "one of the words put out [by the Dukakis campaign] is that he is a rich man—two rich men." And Leslie Stahl said, "The Dukakis campaign was fast out of the box today feeding us such information as the fact that Quayle voted against the plant closing bill, against some civil rights legislation, and for freezing social security." Moments later Dan Rather called Quayle "a rock hard conservative," picked up on those same three votes in his analysis and concluded "he's going to have problems" with them.

CBS variously described the Democrats as "ecstatic," "delighted," and "gleeful" at the prospect of the wealthy conservative adding to the "elitist," country club image of the Republican party. Dukakis' campaign manager Susan Estrich pointedly said they were "very pleased" with Bush's choice, of "J. Danforth Quayle"; and Dan Rather soon adopted that usage for his nightly newscast. Calling it "a victory for the right wing," Estrich pointedly added, "we expected someone better known, with more national stature."

---

[25]Jack Nelson and Richard Meyer, "Bush Selects Quayle as Running Mate," *Los Angeles Times*, August 17, 1988; Walter Robinson and Diane Alters, "Quayle of Indiana is Bush's Choice; Conservative Senator 41, Hailed As 'Innovative,'" *Boston Globe*, August 17, 1988; Curtis Wilkie, "Career in Congress has Won Little Notice," *Boston Globe*, August 17, 1988.

The Democrats were described by Susan Spencer as "scratching their heads and wondering what they're missing"—that is, what there was to be said in favor of Dan Quayle. "The catch phrase I heard over and over today" Mark Shields said on Wednesday evening, "is 'Michael Dukakis is the luckiest SOB in the world!'"[26] Democratic luck went beyond the choice of Dan Quayle to the emerging journalistic profile of Dan Quayle—for which the Democrats could take at least some credit themselves.

There were plenty of positive comments being made about Quayle—more even than the negative ones, according to a published content analysis.[27] But they came sporadically either from loyal convention delegates or from campaign "spin doctors," neither of whom were accorded credibility by the working press. Especially since the positive, Republican comments did not come packaged for easy consumption by a journalistic community looking for thematic coherence. And looking, according to their occupational stance, with a very critical eye. And that meant looking for weaknesses and probing for potential negatives. That is why they were especially receptive to Democratic suggestions. That is why they followed up every negative—expending far more air time and print space on the totally unconfirmed Paula Parkinson episode, for example, than the totally confirmable JTPA performance.[28]

There was, in my view, one more dimension to the early behavior of the journalistic community. And it stems from my sense, mentioned earlier, that reporters who cover politics full-time develop their own preferences in politicians. They like—as do political scientists—those who are good interviews, people who are informative and forthcoming. And among the good interviews, they especially value politicians with whom they have established a comfortable, reliable, day-to-day relationship. But the establishment of day-to-day relationships depends also, I believe, on finding personal or occupational compatibilities with a politician that go further than a mere willingness to talk. By that I mean such things as similar backgrounds or common values or common experiences or mutual respect. Dan Quayle had spent 12 years in Congress. Yet he had remained unknown to the journalistic community. In a sense, they had already made a tentative judgment about him—that nothing they could see on the surface had attracted them to him, and that he was not among their preferred legislative politicians.

---

[26]Transcript, MacNeil/Lehrer Newshour, August 17, 1988.

[27]Center for Media and Public Affairs, "Quayle Hunt: TV News Coverage of the Quayle Nomination," *Media Monitor*, September 1988.

[28]In the five early profiles examined earlier, for example, the Parkinson story consumed 21 column inches or 10 percent of the stories, compared to 7½ column inches and 3 percent for JTPA. On Tuesday, August 23rd, both CBS and ABC led off their evening news with the Parkinson story.

When Bush picked Quayle, however, the journalists were forced into a hasty shot gun marriage. Having not to that point thought him worthy of their attention, they had to get to know him instantly. Necessarily that meant superficially. And superficially, there were very few compatibilities or commonalities on which to launch a comfortable, mutually respectful relationship. Dan Quayle was very young; he was very rich; he was very good looking; he was very conservative; he came from a family of very conservative newspaper publishers; he had frittered away much of his educational opportunity in college; he spent a lot of time playing golf at country clubs; he had not endured any visible hardships in life; he was not introspective; he was not an intellectual; he had no particular verbal or literary skills; he was not comfortable in publicity-seeking situations. It would be hard to create a less likely candidate for immediate journalistic empathy or sympathy or respect or approbation. In all these particulars, except perhaps his age—which was no help to him—Dan Quayle lived across a cultural divide from the members of the community who were about to judge him. If one wanted to prescribe a sitting duck target for a community of political reporters who were rushing to judgment, one could hardly have improved upon J. Danforth Quayle.

I believe there was a cultural—almost a tribal—element in their early reception and treatment of him. The harshness of their language, the relish with which they employed it, the alacrity with which they began, and the certainty with which they wrote suggest to me an exaggerated degree of suspicion, one bordering on disdain and fostering a disinclination to give him any benefit of the doubt. I do not know how much weight to give this tribal rejection, but I do believe it helped to keep the journalists from taking a hard look at his substantive legislative accomplishments—which depended, after all, on their appreciation of a *very different* set of personal attributes—Quayle's political pragmatism, his problem-solving enthusiasm and his coalition building talents. These were political-legislative-governing talents; and they were not the object of journalistic interest or investigation.

Consensus

During the first couple of days, then, the reporters seemed to have no incentive to explore any positives. In time, of course, they might. But the problem, from Quayle's standpoint, was that first he began somewhere below ground zero with the press, second, their emerging thematic consensus was predominantly negative, and third, the consensus was already so solid that it was hard to see what new infusion of information could change it or which journalists would even try. After two days, it had become the path of least resistance for the press to strengthen the consensus by talking to each other and to those outside "sources" who would support it. From my perspective, it is not so much a matter of apportioning weights to various factors as it is a matter of following a process and recording a rapidly accumulating, mutually reenforcing body of information and judgment that precluded the development of any dissonant, alternative views.

If it was at least possible to contemplate a change after the first couple of days, it became impossible to do so after 10 days. In that short span of time, Dan Quayle had been, to the satisfaction of the journalistic community, thoroughly tested and found wanting. Their early consensus was reenforced, confirmed, and cast in brass. A journalistic search for the JTPA story—which I had deemed a certainty several days earlier—was now unimaginable. Their themes and their consensus had combined to preclude the examination of his public record.

Beyond any doubt, Quayle himself was partly responsible. The first and most important public event of his testing time came at a Wednesday morning press conference held before 500 or so hungry journalists who had been waiting all week for the vice presidential story to break and who could not wait to begin testing him. Introducing Quayle, Bush said that "He distinguished himself in the Senate as the author of the Job Training Partnership Act." But there were no questions about that subject. Instead, the questions focused on his pre-Senate resume. Given a chance, however, to put a dent in the emerging consensus, Quayle failed. It was, of course, like nothing else he had ever encountered—and his lack of preparation, his lack of seasoning in national politics was evident.[29] Several of his answers seemed not sufficiently reflective or forthcoming and left obvious holes into which the journalists could be expected to poke and probe further. Which they did—beginning with what Elizabeth Brackett called "a pounding in the network anchor booths" that evening.[30] Journalistic judgment on Quayle's two performances turned decidedly negative, and that in turn stimulated their investigative instincts.

But only on the personal side of things. By Thursday evening, the press was in full and hot pursuit of several stories about the candidate's personal, pre-Senate career—his decision to join the National Guard, his academic record, his sex life. These stories held the journalistic community—reporters and editors—in complete thrall for nearly 10 days, calling them back to their established roles as self-appointed national character cops, which they had already played with such effect in the Gary Hart and Joe Biden cases. For Quayle it meant concentrated and unremitting media scrutiny. Their new found story was made in media heaven—a high stakes drama of a national candidate on public trial for his political life. It was a drama at once intensely personal and broadly

---

[29]See Meg Greenfield, "In the Glare," *Washington Post*, August 19, 1988.
[30]Transcript, MacNeil/Lehrer Newshour, August 18, 1988.

political, holding first the possibility of his withdrawal from the ticket and then the possibility that his very presence on the ticket would cause the defeat of his party's presidential candidate.

On Thursday reported the *New York Times*, "the evening newscasts opened with the controversy over Mr. Quayle's military service, and each program devoted a third or more of its air time to discussing his service in the Guard and the possible damage to the Republican ticket."[31] Tom Brokaw called it "high political drama" and framed the coverage this way:

> There are larger questions here, questions of privilege.
> At a time when a lot of young men from blue collar
> neighborhoods were going to Vietnam, how did this rich
> young man get into the National Guard when there was a
> waiting list? Questions of character (arose) when he didn't
> address those questions last night.

The earlier theme of a nominee's family wealth and power was being elaborated into a story line much more complex, more controversial, and more attention getting—rich young man uses family influence to avoid service in Vietnam. The new theme involved not just money and power, but the use of it, together with ingredients of personal morality and social class—not to mention political consequences. Very quickly, too, the threads of Quayle's conservatism were woven into the new theme as his Senate record of military hawkishness led to allegations of hypocrisy for his failure to serve on active duty.

The new story line led journalists away from Washington and out to Indiana to investigate his personal background and resume. The *New York Times* reported on Friday that "hundreds of reporters were investigating various aspects of Mr. Quayle's record in Indiana."[32] One of his most diligent detractors spoke of "search[ing] thousands of clippings at the *Indianapolis Star and News*."[33] Press scrutiny in Indiana quickly surfaced stories about his academic record, and soon all sorts of obliging sources—like political science professors—came forward to buttress the picture of a privileged, influence-seeking, rich playboy. "The view we had of him," said one DePauw professor, "[was] a corner cutter, a manipulator, an apple polisher, a kid who tried to get by on looks and family connections."[34] His grades, though never released, were reported to be

---

[31]Michael Oreskes, "Convention Message is Garbled By Quayle Static," *New York Times*, August 19, 1988.

[32]R. W. Apple, Jr., "Bush Promises 30 Million Jobs, Pledges Never To Raise Taxes; Backs Quayle Despite Dispute," *New York Times*, August 19, 1988.

[33]Michael Kranish, "In Congress, Quayle Offered Bills to Curb Strikes and Oil Firms," *Boston Globe*, August 23, 1988.

[34]Richard Mayer and Henry Weinstein, "Privilege, Wealth Shaped Quayle," *Los Angeles Times*, August 20, 1988.

poor, adding to the idea that he was a lightweight. And he was said to have needed family influence to get into law school as well as the National Guard—further knitting the idea of privilege to the idea of lightweight. Every new question seemed to reenforce and round out the negative views with which the reporters had begun. They had a dramatic script, and central casting had given them an opportunity to do some full scale character development.

On Saturday, the press corps, frustrated by Quayle's refusal to grant interviews since Wednesday, followed him to hold a loud, boisterous confrontational press conference in his home town in Indiana. On television, it presented a fox and hounds picture, with the journalistic pack cornering and questioning a beleaguered candidate, while his supporters booed and jeered in the background. It could easily be interpreted as a pictorial rendering of current journalistic sentiment—overwhelming, aggressive, unfriendly, and negative. "Those reporters," said Jim Lehrer, "(were) coming on like dogs after the red meat."[35] The next day, reported the *Los Angeles Times*, "Quayle found himself skewered for breakfast on [the Sunday] morning news shows."[36] "The pack" was in full cry, everywhere.

From the press point of view, they were simply following their investigative instincts. They believed they had a story and they were tracking it down wherever it led. "Yesterday, all day," wrote the *Washington Post* on Friday, "nothing was interesting but the story of Dan Quayle and his military career. Reporters were obsessed with it. Quayle's responses to Wednesday night questions galvanized the throng. Here was a story. Here was some suspense. Here in a word, was News."[37] For about 10 days there was an extraordinary concentration of investigative effort poured into what became known as "The Quayle hunt."[38] It was intense enough to affect the reputations of some of the hunters—both individual newspapers and individual reporters.[39] It was a personal, precongressional, private life centered, Indiana-based story; and it preempted all the energy and talent that might have been available to

---

[35]Transcript, The MacNeil/Lehrer Newshour, August 19, 1988.

[36]Bob Sector, "Quayle Flap Will Linger Dole Says: Kansan Predicts Skepticism Among Reagan Democrats," *Los Angeles Times*, August 21, 1988.

[37]Marjorie Williams, "For the Press Pack, Feverish Pursuit and Endless Speculation," *Washington Post*, August 19, 1988.

[38]Eleanor Randolph, "'Quayle Hunt' Turns News Media Into Target for Angry Public," *Washington Post*, August 25, 1988.

[39]The paper was the *Cleveland Plain Dealer*. See Eleanor Randolph, "Quashing a Quayle Rumor," *Washington Post*, August 19, 1988. The reporter was Ellen Hume. See Joan Ennochi, "A Press Insider Steps Out for a Look," *Boston Globe*, January 9, 1989.

pursue a public life, senatorial, JTPA-centered, Washington-based story.

On Thursday the 18th, for example, the *Boston Globe* assigned eight reporters to the story. They wrote 7 articles on Dan Quayle, only one of which even mentioned JTPA. Their articles plus 4 op ed pieces—all negative in tone—consumed 187 column inches, only 2½" of which—less than 2 percent—mentioned JTPA. In the *New York Times* on Friday the 19th, 5 reporters and 2 columnists produced 118 column inches on Dan Quayle, but they contained no mention at all of his senatorial accomplishments. That same day, the *Washington Post* assigned 15 reporters to the story and produced 232 column inches, in 5 stories and 4 columns—all unfavorable to Quayle. On Sunday the 21st, the *Los Angeles Times* had 15 reporters mentioning Dan Quayle adversely in 11 different stories—not to mention 4 negative columnists and 2 negative cartoons. Of the total of 251 column inches on the campaign, 142 column inches (57 percent) were devoted to Quayle. And there was not one mention of JTPA. The journalistic community, "the pack," was being driven by expectations of finding a very different story.

Six new Quayle profiles—in the *New York Times, Washington Post, Los Angeles Times, Boston Globe, Time,* and *Newsweek*—consumed a total of 299 column inches, only 7" of which were devoted to JTPA. That is 2 percent of the total coverage, or one inch of coverage for every 40 column inches of print. That is a small decline in what was already a minuscule amount of attention in the five earlier profiles. But it is consistent with the notion that the National Guard and academic record stories pulled journalistic attention even further away from his performance in the Senate. The headlines of these six, second-stage profiles were indicative of their focus:

"Dan Quayle: A Life of Contrasts: Nomination Puts Focus on Candidate's Younger Days" (*Boston Globe* 8/21/88)

"World of Advantage Made a Sturdy Ladder for Quayle to Climb to Success" (*New York Times* 8/26/88)

"Privilege, Wealth Shaped Quayle" (*Los Angeles Times* 8/21/88)

"From Political Pretty Boy to Running Mate" (*Washington Post Weekly National Edition* 8/22-28/88)

"Who is Dan Quayle?" (*Newsweek* 8/29/88)

"Family, Golf and Politics" (*Time* 8/29/88)

Neither the *Globe* nor the *LA Times* profiles mentioned JTPA. The *Washington Post* cut the length of their mention in half; the *New York Times* increased theirs. *Newsweek* mentioned it only in their next to last and last paragraphs saying, "Quayle is probably best known for his sponsorship, with Ted Kennedy "of JTPA, saying that it was "better structured than CETA," and concluded, "but Quayle had it funded at relatively low levels." *Time* listed JTPA dead last, as eleventh in a list of eleven Senate activities. No highlighting there. If anything, this second spate of profiles increased the proportion of coverage devoted to Quayle's pre-Senate, private life—driving JTPA even further from view. And, in the articles that did focus directly on his Senate record, JTPA remained a very minor element. In a pair of additional articles devoted specifically to Quayle's Senate record in the *New York Times*, for example, two veteran congressional reporters devoted 68 inches to their subject, with 3½" or 5 percent devoted to JTPA.[40] That was a small increase in coverage over the profiles, but hardly elevating the accomplishment to a level of importance where anyone would be stimulated to notice. A similar article on his Senate record in the *Washington Post*, by another experienced Capitol Hill reporter, yielded 1½ inches, or 7 percent of a 21" column.[41] Quayle's major senatorial accomplishment was not being treated as major anywhere within the journalistic community.

The weekend of August 28-29 marked the end of the feverish "Quayle hunt." The precongressional story had run its course to no authoritative conclusion on the issues that had been raised. On the 27th, the story left the front page of the sharply negative *Boston Globe* for the first time. On the 28th, media analyst Robert Lichter closed down his study of Quayle's treatment on the nightly news, because Quayle stories had ended.[42] On the 29th, the *New York Times* reporter who first broke the story of Quayle's vice-presidential prospects wrote, "There may be little more to ask about the Indiana senator's national guard service, grades or resume...."[43] Editors broke up the pack by dispersing their reporters to other stories. As quickly as it had formed, the pack disappeared.

At the same time, the 10-day performance of the press came under self-scrutiny. On the 28th the *Globe* published a highly self-critical analysis of "Quayle's treatment at the hands of an accusatory press." "There has been little to commend and much to condemn," wrote Walter Robinson, "in the ferocious public inquiry into Quayle's background."[44] On that same day, the *Los Angeles Times* produced a critical review of media performance. "Quayle has become the subject of a clamorous national character hunt.... In the process, the press gangly and club-footed gum shoe that it is—has become part of the story.... Has the press botched the job?" asked Thomas Rosensteil. "If so, was it because of some liberal bias?

---

[40]Steven Roberts, "Quayle Works to Overcome Early Image," *New York Times*, August 18, 1988; Martin Tolchin, "Quayle's Record in Senate Reflects Fervently Held Conservative Views," *New York Times*, August 29, 1988.

[41]Helen Dewar, "Battle Lines Form Over Quayle's Record," *Washington Post*, August 18, 1988.

[42]See note 27, *supra*.

[43]Gerald Boyd, "Question of Selection," *New York Times*, August 29, 1988.

[44]Walter Robinson, "Quayle Hunt Has a Whiff of Hypocrisy: Senator Asked to Carry a Generation's War Guilt," *Boston Globe*, August 28, 1988.

And has the press really appointed itself the national character cop?" He keyed his article to the *Times-Mirror* poll, which had found that 55 percent of the respondents felt the press treatment of Quayle was "unfair" and 60 percent felt there was "too much coverage."[45]

A week later, Robert Lichter published the results of his study of the evening news' treatment of Quayle. He found that the Quayle hunt "took up more than one-quarter of all evening news broadcasts for nearly two weeks after his nomination." He also found a backlash against the media. "When the press takes on the role of political opposition," he wrote "the electorate may reject the messenger as well as the message."[46] Perhaps, in its singleminded pursuit of "the story" and in its concern for the dramatic, it had lost touch with its audience. The *Washington Post's* ombudsman wrote a staff memo, along those lines, strongly criticizing that paper's Quayle coverage. "We still find it difficult to resist the mob psychology that seizes the press corps on occasion," he wrote. "Part of that psychology is to seek validation in the actions and decisions of competitors. If 'the networks' do it, it must be right and true...in our eagerness to not be left behind, we succumbed to the soiled embrace of Paula Parkinson."[47] These commentaries speak for themselves.

I cite this cluster of events to indicate that the media's intense first look at Dan Quayle was over. We are also reminded, by the press's own reaction, of just how intense that scrutiny had been. So intense, I believe, that it effectively completed the picture of Dan Quayle. The self-criticism of the press speaks for itself in terms of their own internal, professional gyroscope. But at that time, none of them offered the JTPA story as a validating external corrective—even with the story still sitting there waiting to be written.

The publication in September of a Labor Department report on the results of JTPA prompted one article each in the *New York Times, Boston Globe, Washington Post,* and *Los Angeles Times.*[48] To one degree or another, each one argued that Quayle's claims for its success were exaggerated. And those experts in the field who were politically opposed to Quayle took this opportunity to weigh in with negative opinions. So

---

[45]Thomas Rosensteil, "Quayle Coverage Puts Spotlight on Media: Has Story Been Botched?" *Los Angeles Times,* August 28, 1988. See also Richard Berke, "55 percent of Voters See Press as Unfair to Quayle," *New York Times,* August 28, 1988.

[46]S. Robert Lichter, "Media Got Singed For Overcooking in Quayle Roast," *Wall Street Journal,* September 7, 1988.

[47]Richard Harwood, memo of September 2, 1988, as published in "Post Memo Assails Its Quayle Overkill," *Washington Times,* September 15, 1988.

[48]Richard Cohen, "Second Fiddles"; Drummond Ayres, "Both Bentsen and Quayle With Fortunes Varying, Display A Sense of Ease," *New York Times,* October 23, 1988.

the overall tone of these articles was uniformly downbeat. And, in any case, they did not treat his legislative leadership except by inference. They didn't help; but they didn't matter. And aside from them, JTPA virtually disappeared from view. It was a case of collective myopia, or collective amnesia, or collective contentment, or all three. The journalists saw no reason to change the story and the drama they had. It was a story they had begun to weave from the moment Quayle's name emerged. And everything from day one had reenforced and elaborated on it.

Nothing that was said or done after those first 10 days added anything or subtracted anything from the negative picture. Dan Quayle never got an updated second look. And he campaigned uphill all the way. Not even Ted Kennedy's JTPA-based assertion that press coverage of Quayle "has not been a fair characterization of him" changed anything.[49] It would be easy to document, if I had time, that the tenor of press commentary remained consistently and contagiously negative. The editorial cartoonists (not to mention the comedians) had long since followed suit by turning him into a national joke—and they were having a field day caricaturing the privileged, influence-seeking, rich boy, the shallow, immature, infelicitous, unaccomplished lightweight. The nation's journalists spent much of the 1988 campaign (and afterward) expressing their collective disappointment, disgust, frustration, disapproval, and rage at the low-level, issueless, unfair, negative, uninformed, personalized quality of the campaign. From my perspective, their own treatment of Dan Quayle contributed substantially to the very characteristics they so earnestly deplored.

All that remained for them to do from the end of August to the end of the campaign, was to speculate as to whether or not Quayle's "negatives" or his "unfavorables" would be sufficiently strong to pull down the top of the ticket. That became their new theme, their final story line on Dan Quayle. The voters of course wrote an end to that one. As he put it when we talked afterwards, "When I went on the ticket, Bush was 17 points down in the polls. After I went on the ticket, he went 12 points ahead in the polls. And we won by 8 points. That's all I know." And he smiled.

---

[49]Kenneth Noble, "Quayle is Proud, and Others Skeptical, of Job Plan," *New York Times*, September 4, 1988; Henry Weinstein and Douglas Frantz, "Experts Question Benefits of Jobs Program," *Los Angeles Times*, September 7, 1988; Michael Kranish, "Beleaguered Job Program Could Be Thorn in Quayle's Side," *Boston Globe*, September 11, 1988; Frank Swoboda, "Job Training Act Earns Raves, Reservations: Quayle Touts 5 Year Old Program, But Cosponsor Kennedy Plays Down Its Impact," *Washington Post*, September 18, 1988.

Comparisons

After my book came out and I started doing TV and radio interviews, I was asked repeatedly whether or not I thought the journalistic treatment of Dan Quayle had been fair. And I would always reply that I thought it was "unbalanced," that it paid too much attention to his precongressional private life and too little to his public life in the Senate. I understood, I said, why they would concentrate first on the personal background of someone they did not know; but I could not understand, I said, why they stopped at that point in his career and did not investigate his later career, his Senate career, with a similar zeal. They acted, I usually added, as if they believed the real key to an assessment of Dan Quayle as a possible vice president was to be found in the Registrar's office at DePauw University rather than in the committee rooms or on the floor of the United States Senate. There has been much self-scrutiny within the journalistic community about the appropriateness of their searches into the private life of public officials.[50] From my perspective, the far more serious aspect of that problem is the neglect of the public life of public officials that seems inevitably to follow.

I have tried here both to describe and to explain from my viewpoint why the journalistic community pretty much neglected something that I had spent three-quarters of a book highlighting. There is, in all of this, the assumption that JTPA is worth a lot of attention. Everything I know about Congress tells me that it is. But this assumption can be tested. We can undertake comparable studies of other legislators and their legislative accomplishments at similar points in their careers. By minimizing JTPA or dismissing it out of hand—and in any case by deciding *not* to study it—the journalistic community acted as if they had in fact done some such comparative research. Yet there is no evidence that they ever had. They operated, it would seem, on a snap judgment. From start to finish, they propounded judgments; but they did not do the work.

I want to avoid the conclusion that they were unfair—though I believe they were—in favor of the broader conclusion that journalists simply behave differently than political scientists. I want further to conclude that we will produce a better balanced, more useful understanding of our politicians than they will. And I want to conclude finally, that we simply cannot expect them to do our job for us.

Above all else, I conclude from this case that it takes time—a lot of time—to render informed and fair judgments about politicians. Time allows us to see politicians in more than one context, to consider growth in matters of responsibility and perspective and ability, to suspend bias and

---

[50]For example, Dom Bonafede, "Scoop or Snoop," *National Journal*, November 11, 1988.

entertain doubt where first impressions are involved. Time allows us to be slow to judge and we should be. It is a set of conditions more easily met by political scientists than by journalists. Indeed, one implication from the Quayle case is that political scientists care more about and are more likely to focus on the *political* activity of politicians than journalists are.

We will, to be sure, produce a different picture than they. In the Quayle case, for example, the subjects to which the journalists devoted the bulk of their time and energy—family wealth, national guard, the academic record, for example, or the influence of his wife—were matters I did not touch at all in my study. I did not encounter them during my field work; and since the friendly Indiana press never pushed hard on them, they never came up. In any case, my effort to discover coherence and patternings in his senatorial activities tended to crowd out a concern for these matters of personal background.

When I called two of my reporter friends in Washington to ask them if they wanted the galleys of my book, one asked "Are there any revelations?" and the other asked "Is there any big news?" No, I said, there wasn't. Never mind they said. After "Good Morning America" had invited me to be on their program, they said, "We're sure you have much to tell us about his private life." When I said I didn't, they withdrew the invitation.

On the other hand, inattention to matters of personal background may have weakened my portrait of Dan Quayle. For I deliberately excluded a few things I did observe, things that might have produced a more personal and less flattering picture than the one I produced. I accept the need to make judgments in withholding private matters that were not intended for me and that could only hurt the individual whose career I am trying to explain—without adding any explanatory power. Such an outlook is perhaps, more akin to the journalistic practices of the 1950s or 1960s than those of the 1980s.

In making such judgments, however, the political scientist differs from the journalist. The politician needs the journalist; the journalist feels no special gratitude for his or her access, and that businesslike relationship allows the journalist greater latitude in delving into personal matters without losing access. The political scientist, on the other hand, knows that he or she is of no use to the politician, feels gratitude for being allowed to observe, develops a more sympathetic relationship, and knows that any excursion into personal matters risks losing future access. The different terms of our bargains with politicians, then, may help account for different pictures of the same politician.

Certainly, too, we operate with different perceptual screens. The case of Quayle's speaking style is a case in point. I would search for meaning or for patterns in what he said, and would overlook his tendency to malapropisms.   The journalists would overlook the substance of his remarks, in their stakeout for verbal gaffes.   Was this because the journalists weight verbal skill more heavily and I weigh coalition building skill more heavily?   Or, was it because their goal was to test, on behalf of the voting public, a candidate for vice president while mine was to describe, on behalf of college students, the career of a sitting U.S. senator?   Or was it because our audiences held different expectations about our product, theirs involving an appetite for drama, mine involving expectations about structure?   Or was it that my overall stance toward Quayle contained larger dosages of sympathy and fewer dosages of suspicion than theirs?   My guess is that all of these matters help explain our differences.   And they are all worth thinking about.

From the evidence of the Dan Quayle case alone, my conclusion is that journalists will come to judgments about politicians too quickly, too superficially, and too inflexibly to fill the political scientists' need for an understanding of politicians.   Their collective rush to judgment, the incompleteness and the lopsidedness of their evidence, and their large swings in attentiveness, give plenty of support for this conclusion. Especially since so much of what they did is explainable by the durable built-in incentives and working conditions of their profession—the competitive drive to get the story, the reliance on easily available sources, the development of short run themes, the audience appetite for personalized and dramatic themes, the homogenizing influence of the pack.

It will take a more patient, more cautious, more thorough, more sustained, more open-minded, more balanced kind of investigation if we are to produce the kind of reliable knowledge about politicians that can be integrated into our generalizations about politics.   There can be neither short cuts nor snap judgments. And moving pictures, rather than candid photos will be required.   It takes a lot of time, a willingness to suspend a lot of biases and beliefs, plus a drive to search widely and test sternly for evidence in order to understand a politician. More of each, I believe, than journalists are likely to produce.

The two professions must and will continue to work the same territory, to talk to each other and contribute to each other's work.   But the journalistic community cannot do our job for us. They did not do it in the Dan Quayle case. They did not even try. That is the bad news and the good news for political scientists who wish to do it themselves.

3

The Political Scientist as
Participant Observer[*]

In a book that urges more scholarly attention to congressional activity outside of Washington, D.C., it might be helpful to say something about how this kind of research is done. This is a kind of research—the study of people in their natural setting—that is not much written about by political scientists. Described in this book as "soaking and poking"—or "just hanging around," it is more formally known as field research, or qualitative research, or—our preference—participant observation.[1] This is

---

[*]From *Home Style: House Members in their Districts*, Boston: Little Brown, 1978, Appendix. Reprinted by permission of Scott Foresman and Company.

[1]Three political scientists who have written helpfully about the subject are: Lewis Anthony Dexter, *Elite and Specialized Interviewing* (Evanston, IL: Northwestern University Press, 1970); Alexander Heard, "Interviewing Southern Politicians," *American Political Science Review* 44 (December 1950): 886-896; and James A. Robinson, "Participant Observation, Political Internships and Research" in *Political Science Annual, Volume* 2, ed. James Robinson (Indianapolis: Bobbs Merrill, 1970), pp. 71-110. The other works I have found most useful are: *Issues in Participant Observation: A Text and a Reader*, eds. George McCall and J. L. Simmons (Reading, MA: Addison-Wesley, 1969); Leonard Schatzman and Anselm Strauss, *Field Research: Strategies for a Natural Sociology* (Englewood Cliffs, NJ: Prentice-Hall, 1973); Barney Glaser and Anselm Strauss, *The Discovery of Grounded Theory:*

a largely autobiographical case study of participant observation, written less about how this kind of research is done than about how one particular research project was done. However, because of the current dearth of understanding of these research methods—in this case a blend of observation, interviewing, and participation—even a case study can have broad benefits.

In the first place, students of Congress may find some instructive comparisons with Washington-based research. There, the typical researcher starts with a set of questions, obtains appointments with some set of legislators, goes to each legislator's office for a 45-minute interview, leaves, and moves on to the next interview. That is what my own experience had been. Many of the problems of research in the district are the same as those encountered on Capitol Hill because, after all, both take place in the milieu of the legislator. But in home district research, one typically watches, listens to, and talks to one congressman morning, noon, and night for several days. This degree of immersion in the natural setting is so great that it is a qualitatively different experience from that on Capitol Hill.

In the second place, political scientists with a general interest in method may find the following comments helpful in bringing participant observation more comfortably under the tent of political science methodology. As long as political scientists continue to study politicians, some of us certainly will want to collect data through repeated interaction with these politicians in their natural habitats. If that is so, we should be as self-conscious as we can be about this kind of political science activity and about the relationship between political scientists and politicians that it entails. And not just because people doing this kind of research can benefit; but also because, through their lack of understanding, political scientists who do not do this kind of research can unintentionally impede the work of those who do.

Furthermore, participant observation does have some method to it. It is difficult to standardize in canonical form—a difficulty that will become exasperatingly obvious in a moment. One can hardly be very pretentious about it. Still, a research project like this one does not just happen; it does not proceed without a degree of planning and care and methodological worry. It is these "worries," perhaps, that are most revealing about any research project. I hope the particular worries of this one will be instructive to those political scientists who like to generalize about methodological worries.

Strategies for Qualitative Research (Chicago: Aldine, 1967); William Foote Whyte, *Street Corner Society*, 2d ed. (Chicago: University of Chicago Press, 1955), Appendix.

Research based on participant observation is likely to have an exploratory emphasis. Someone doing this kind of research is quite likely to have no crystallized idea of what he or she is looking for or what questions to ask when he or she starts. Researchers typically become interested in some observable set of activities and decide to go have a firsthand look at them. They fully expect that an open minded exposure to events in the milieu and to the perspectives of those with whom they interact will produce ideas that might never have occurred to them otherwise. Only after prolonged, unstructured soaking is the problem formulated. Indeed, the reformulation of a problem or a question may be the end product of the research. The idea of home style had never occurred to me until I had taken quite a few trips around the country. I had been interested in a very different set of questions when I began my travels—questions of perception and questions relating these perceptions to behavior on Capitol Hill, especially roll call voting. I was not at all interested in the effect of perceptions on behavior in the district. In other words, participant observation seems less likely to be used to test an existing hypothesis than to formulate hypotheses for testing by others or to uncover some relationship that strikes others as worth hypothesizing about. It may be an appropriate method, however, at *any* stage of a research endeavor where there is a felt need for a fresh line of thought.

This particular project was undertaken for several reasons. Like any other political scientist interested in representative-constituent relations, I had been teaching the received wisdom on the subject. Part of that wisdom tells us that the representative's perception of his or her constituency is an important variable. But, in the absence of much empirical exposition of such perceptions and in the presence of politicians who seemed less than cognizant of all segments of their "constituency," I had been telling students that the subject—like dozens of others—deserved "further research." Someone, I kept saying, should address the perceptual question: What does a member of Congress see when he or she sees a constituency? The decision to be that someone was made, however, partly because the perceptual question seemed researchable by a method I had used before and with which I felt especially secure—the personal interview. The interview method was not the only method available, but it was appropriate to the question I wanted to answer. Had it not been for the appropriateness of a familiar method, the perceptual question would undoubtedly have been left for someone else.

I had no idea what kinds of answers I would get. I had no idea what questions to ask. I knew only that I wanted to get some House members to talk about their constituency perceptions—up and down and all around the subject. I knew that I had had some practice talking to legislators and that if I had developed any professional skills as a political scientist it was as an interviewer of, and a listener to, politicians. My hope was that I

57

might be able to piece together their perceptions, categorize them in some way, and generalize about them. The decision to interview, to watch, and to listen *in the districts* was made simultaneously with the decision to do the research. I thought that if I could see what they saw in the district at the same time they saw it, I could better understand their perceptual statements. I could not only listen, I could listen in context. I could check what I heard *from* them with what I observed *with* them—something I could not do in a Capitol Hill office interview.

There were other reasons for doing this research in this way. First, all my previous research had been conducted in Washington, from a Washington perspective. I knew intellectually that activity in Washington reflects to some uncertain degree what people are saying, thinking, and doing out in the country; but I felt I did not know what went on "out there." I wanted to acquire, at first hand, this extra-Washington perspective. Indeed, in the early months of the research, I spoke of myself primarily as a traveler, as a John Steinbeck without a camper or a "Charlie." Thus, the research question appealed to me partly because the research site—the country—appealed to me.

As a sometime Congress-watcher, I also felt that interviews were becoming increasingly difficult to get in Washington, as more and more researchers descended on the Capitol and as senators and representatives felt beset by ever more burdensome job demands. I had then (and I have now) no doubt whatever that good interviews can be obtained on Capitol Hill. But a personal reaction I had had to the increasing difficulty was to wonder whether a better quality interview might not be had—irrespective of subject matter—if the legislator could be approached in some setting other than the Capitol Hill office. Because of my interest in perceptions, a constituency interview seemed particularly appealing. The member's view of a constituency, I guessed, would take shape mainly *in the constituency* rather than in Washington. Furthermore, it would probably take shape within many different contexts within each constituency. So, the more contexts I could place the member in, the richer would be the perspectives he or she would communicate to me. The standard Capitol Hill interview captures the legislator at one point in time, in one mood, in one response set, in one interaction; a few days in the district, however, might yield a variety of such contextual factors. Besides, it seemed, the House member might just have more time to talk and be more relaxed in the home environment. All this seemed plausible—that interview *quality* might be better in the home setting. The opportunity to test this hunch gave the project added appeal.

Finally, once the idea seemed appealing enough to undertake "sometime," it was clear that the time had to be soon. Not to start immediately might mean I would never do it. Field research on Congress is a young person's game. It requires a degree of physical stamina and psychological adaptability that, taken together, are optimized in people of their twenties and thirties more than in their forties and fifties (even though people in their forties do have the advantage of being closer to the average age of House members). So I figured that I had better get going before I became too weary or too inflexible to tolerate the discomforts endemic to this type of data-grubbing operation.

The "Sample"

Once the decision was made to do the research, the question became: Whom should I observe? This is, somewhat elegantly, the sample problem. My answer at the beginning was, I don't know; my answer today is, I'm not sure. Nothing better characterizes the open-ended, slowly emerging, participant observation research than this admission. If I had been certain about what types of representatives and what types of districts to sample, I would already have had answers to a lot of the questions raised in this book. My procedure was slowly to build up the size of the group being observed and constantly to monitor its composition to see what commonly recognized types of members or districts I might be neglecting. Then I would move to remedy any imagined deficiencies. I spent a lot of time trying to figure out a priori what types of members or districts might post serious tests for, or exceptions to, whatever generalizations seemed to be emerging—with the intent of bringing such members or districts into the group. At one point, I noticed there were too many lawyers; the next two people I chose were nonlawyers. At another point, I had been traveling with a string of younger members; the next one I chose was a House veteran. My *Almanac of American Politics* is dogeared from constant thumbing; my note folders are still thick with tentative, revised, and re-revised lists of prospective traveling companions. Articles about congressional politics and congressional elections, census statistics, the *Congressional Record* were read with an eye to the adequacy of the current "sample." Do I have one of these? Should I? What is the marginal value of one of these as opposed to one of those? In 1974 I pursued a target of opportunity, by loading up on Republicans whom I could watch explain their impeachment vote. By the time I reached their districts, however, the need to explain had evaporated; and I had to use two House members not in my group as examples. As a result, the group remains unrepresentatively Republican (10 Democrats, 8 Republicans).

Of course, in no technical sense do I have a sample. But I did not make a decision to travel with any member without first assessing or reassessing the characteristics he or she might add to the group and without comparing each addition with several other possibilities. Each person added to the list represented a heavy commitment of my time, energy, and money, so no decision was made lightly. And no decision was made quickly. In 1970 the group numbered 4, in 1972 it jumped to 12, in 1974 it went to 16, and in 1976 it stopped at 18. Decisions were made deliberately, but on the basis of limited information, by incremental, successive comparison. The decision to stop at 18 was arbitrary, occasioned not by the thought that the "sample" was complete, but by the thought that it was about time to stop running around and to begin to communicate what I was finding.

I tried to assemble a variety of House members and districts. I have also tried to make it clear that no claims are being made for the representativeness of the group—only for its adequacy in opening up the subject for scholarly inquiry.

One nonobvious criterion worth mentioning is "receptivity to academics." During my previous research on Congress, I formulated a heuristic proposition: there are only two classes of legislators in the world—"good interviews" and "bad interviews." There is a great temptation to apply this proposition to district research by saying, "I'll only travel with people I already know are articulate, responsive, and comfortable with academics." But if I do that, if I limit my group to "good interviews," won't that produce bias? The easy way out would be to avoid the pain of dealing with people who are suspicious of academics, difficult to reach, and difficult to interview. But at what price? Once, I wrote to a political science friend asking him to recommend which of two House members from his state I should select. He recommended one on the grounds that he was well regarded by the local political scientists. He called the other "a clunk...who had made no impression here." I decided to go with the "clunk," precisely because he had a style that seemed unappealing to academics. By recognizing a variation on the receptivity problem, I was able to offset it. And I was able to formulate a second heuristic proposition. Beware of political scientists bearing gifts of access. In the end, 7 of the 18 members were people who were used to and comfortable with academics, 6 were neither accustomed to nor comfortable with academics, and 5 were somewhere in between on this version of the at-homeness index.

It is an obvious characteristic of this project, and of participant observation research generally, that it deals with a small number of cases. It is the "small N" that makes this type of research unamenable to statistical analysis. At the point in the project when I had traveled with 12 members, I gave much thought to collaborating with another political scientist and interviewing a much larger, more reliable sample of House members, one that would give us the chance to do some statistical analysis. I finally decided that I did not yet feel confident that I knew what to ask in such a survey-type questionnaire, and that I preferred, for the time being, to proceed with the study of a few cases. It was a deliberate decision to sacrifice analytical range for analytical depth. It was also a decision that placed severe limits on the number of members who could be studied—20, no more than 25. The problem is one of span of control, the control of one mind. Each case must be known in depth. Regular contact with each member must be maintained. As a matter of fact, I never did keep in as close contact as I wished. But the desire not to fall too far out of touch set limits to the size of the group. So, too, did financial and professional constraints. This kind of research is both costly and hard to finance. And I could not get away from the classroom as often as would be necessary to travel personally with very many members.

Table A charts the 36 trips made to the various districts between 1970 and 1977. It also charts the spacing between visits to each of the 18 members. As noted in the Introduction, the vast majority of the trips were made in election years; mostly in the fall. That was the easiest time to catch members at home, to parlay consecutive visits, and to observe in the greatest number of contexts.

It may have distorted my view of home activity by giving it an intensity it might not have had during another part of the electoral cycle. In some cases, that was surely true. But the out-of-season visits displayed the same variations in intensity as the in-season ones, leading me to guess that generalization about seasonal effects would be hazardous. The chart clearly shows, however, that one watches certain people at certain times of their lives and their careers. If I had come earlier or returned later, each individual might have shown a different face, a different home style. If I had come at some period other than 1970 to 1977, member attacks on their institution might not have been so strong; or, the members might not have placed so much emphasis on access. I cannot know. The book's conclusions about individuals and the group are time-bound and cannot be cast in brass. They are only a best estimate—at the time.

Access

I made contact with my prospects in two ways—a personal contact of some sort or "cold turkey." The first four members I took on as an experiment in 1970 were all people with whom I had had some contact—two from my previous research, one whose administrative assistant I knew, and one for whom an undergraduate student of mine was working as an intern. In 10 of the next 14 cases, I wrote a "cold turkey" letter. Here is that standard letter:

> Dear Representative_____,
>
> I am writing to ask if you might be willing to let me travel around with you when you are in your district for a three- or four-day period sometime this spring. I am a professor of political science at the University of Rochester and am writing a book on the relations

Table A Timing and Spacing of District Visits

	Jan.	Feb.	March	April	May	June	July	August	Sept.	Oct.	Nov.	Dec.	Totals Trips	Days
1970						A[a]-3[b]				B-3[c] A-2 C-3	D-4		5	15
1971					A-2 C-3								2	5
1972				E-3	F-2		G-2 H-3 I-3		D-4	J-5 K-4 L-3			9	29
1973													0	0
1974						F-3	G-2		M-4 I-4	N-3 O-3 J-2 H-4 B-3 A-4		P-2	11	34
1975													0	0
1976		N-3		P-3	Q-4				C-3	M-3 R-3 D-3			7	22
1977					Q-3 O-2								2	5
Totals Trips	0	1	0	2	6	2	4	0	4	15	1	1	36	
Days	0	3	0	6	16	6	10	0	15	48	4	2		110

[a] Representatives are given identifying letters (A, B, etc.) in the order in which I visited their districts. These letters bear *no relation* to the letters given to representatives in the text.

[b] The number opposite the representative's identifying letter is the number of working days I spent in the district on that particular trip. It does not include traveling time except when I accompanied the member on an active schedule on the same day I traveled.

[c] Within any given month, I have preserved the order in which I took the trips.

between congressmen and their constituencies. I'm trying to learn about the subject by accompanying a dozen or so House members as they work in their districts.

About myself: I am 45-years-old and have been writing in the field of American politics for a number of years.   Books I have written include *The President's Cabinet*, 1959; *National Politics and Federal Aid to Education*, 1962; *The Power of the Purse: Appropriations Politics in Congress*, 1966; and *Congressmen in Committees*, 1973.

Needless to say, I'd be tremendously pleased if you could see your way clear to letting me accompany you in

_____.

Of course, all of this would be entirely at my own expense.   I could even come to Washington should you wish to talk with me about it in person.   I look forward to hearing from you and thank you in advance for your consideration of this request.

Sincerely,

To this letter, I sometimes added, as a personal reference, the name of one or two members I had already traveled with—members with whom the new prospect might have ties.   Thus, I pyramided later trips on the foundation of earlier ones.   I know of one case in which that personal reference was essential.   But I have no idea how many people took me purely on the face value of the request.

I had two outright refusals.   One was from a powerful senior member whom I had met and who had reportedly lost touch with his district—a type I do not have in my group.   He said he wasn't going to do any campaigning—that he had no opponent and that his wife was very ill.   The second refusal came from a member who wrote,

I think you would find my kind of activity dull, boring, and completely unworthy of your time.   I am sure you have a limited amount of time, and I feel you ought to devote it to those areas wherein some of our more dramatic members do their work.   Accordingly, while I deeply appreciate your interest, I must respectfully decline the opportunity to work with you on your project.

My best guess is that he is suspicious of academics.   There is the possibility in some cases that my letter, in which I present myself as an academic, will trigger a strongly negative reaction.

Arranging a visit to the district is not always easy—mostly because the plans of House members are subject to sudden changes.   I prefer to plan

63

for and schedule specific blocks of time or dates well in advance. The members' tendency was to say "keep in touch and we'll work something out—maybe about the middle of September." So I would have to place an entire two or three week period "on hold" to accommodate a member. Rather than send out many letters at once—as one would do before heading for a two-week stay in Washington—I had to dribble them out in ones or twos. If distances and expenses were great, and I wanted to coordinate a couple of trips, the representatives' vagueness made planning doubly difficult. In California, I chose the Republican member partly by asking the administrative assistant of my California Democrat which Republican assistants he got along with, so that *they* could negotiate across offices for a time for a single California visit.

In nearly half of the cases, I had some scheduling choice; someone on the member's staff would read me the itinerary for two or three trips home and ask me to choose. When that happened, I opted for the dates that promised to let me observe the greatest number of events, settings, and locales; and I avoided dates where events—like conventions or lengthy meetings or totally unscheduled days—promised to keep me separated from the congressman.

Logistically, the research was always subject to uncertainty. One morning, I had my bag packed and was planning to leave for the airport in 20 minutes when the congressman's secretary called to say the deal was off; it was the congressman's birthday, and his wife did not want any outsider around during the festivities. On one occasion, when I had arranged to fly back to Washington with the congressman and had saved up some questions, I overslept and missed the plane entirely—an example of what experimentalists would call "instrument decay."

In this kind of research, which brings you into face-to-face working relationships with influential political people, there needs to be some mutual understanding about the relationships—its boundaries, its proprieties, its exchanges. Because you approach each other as strangers, this mutual understanding is worked out very gradually. It is useful to think of this relationship as a *bargain* between two professionals.

For my part, I began by presenting myself as a serious scholar, with a long-term professional interest in studying Congress. I came seeking information with which to write a book, information that I could not get anywhere else but from them. I presented as little as possible about the details of my project—only the few words necessary to justify a trip to the district, nothing more. My initial commitments were professional, and were unrelated to research content. If, in the letter, I gave the name of another member as a reference, the only quality I suggested they might wish to check on was my "personal integrity." Implicitly, I agreed, as a professional scholar, not to write an exposé, not to kiss and tell, not to cause a member personal or political damage, not to quote a member when he or she wished not to be quoted. It was my hope that if I presented myself as a professional, they would realize that I have high standards to uphold and that my career, *just as much as theirs*, would be placed in jeopardy if I did not keep my end of the bargain.

As for what the projected book was all about, each member formed his own idea of that. Each wanted only to be able to explain to his constituents why I was accompanying him. "He's come to see how we do it here in southern Illinois." "He's writing a book about how members of Congress campaign back home and has chosen this district to study. If we behave ourselves, we may become a footnote." "He's writing a book about how members of Congress deal with their constituents, and he's using me as a guinea pig. As I understand it, he'll write a book of 500 to 600 pages whose only buyer will be the Library of Congress—and his students. That's what professors do, you know, when they aren't grading papers." "He's collecting a lot of information. I don't know what he'll do with it. But he likes to watch these things. He doesn't bother the women and he doesn't talk too much." A detailed outline of what I was doing was not essential to our bargain. It was almost beside the point. Even when I answered their subsequent (but infrequent) probes by telling them that I was interested in the perceptual question, they continued to internalize and to describe my subject in behavioral terms (i.e., "campaigning," "how we do it," "dealing with constituents," etc.) rather than perceptual terms. This reaction encourages me to think that the perceptual question is, indeed, a political science question. It is not one politicians naturally think about or generalize about.

For their part, why would they enter into this bargain at all? Why would they agree to subject themselves to a presence and a scrutiny that was at best a nuisance and brought no very striking benefits? I was, after all, one of a horde of supplicants—people who wanted something from them. Probably their reasons were varied. For some, the visit may have been a welcome change in the routine, something different. They spend their lives reaching out to include different people within their orbit; and, if they do not normally associate with academics or writers, the opportunity for closer contact with such a person may interest them. For some, acceptance may have been a conditioned reflex. They are used to having journalists ask to interview them, and they view such requests as something that goes with the job. Some may have seen it as part of their civic duty to educate teachers of politics. Some may enjoy attention from whatever quarter—the more so because, compared to senators, they attract so little outside interest. They live by publicity and may deem any chance to get some, however remote, worth an inconvenience. For some, scholarly attention may be flattering, the more so when the scholar comes as a student who wants to learn from them rather than as a professor who wants to instruct them. For some, even, the prospect of an academic amanuensis may have stirred acceptance. Some House members would like to be immortalized between book covers; and political scientists are among the gatekeepers to book covers. For one or more, or none, of these reasons perhaps, they agreed to take me on.

Whatever their reasons, they were all completely confident of their ability to protect themselves. As part of the bargain—which I sometimes mentioned explicitly—they could exclude me from any event they wished. House members are, moreover, well practiced in talking for the record. They are, in short, professionals just as I am a professional. My confidence in my ability to get them to talk was matched by their confidence in their ability to say nothing they did not wish to say. If we were equally good at our businesses, the result would not be a disaster for either of us. Thus, from their point of view, although there might be no big gain from my visit, there would be no big loss either.

When you talk with members of Congress and when you write up your research you are especially aware of acting as a representative of the scholarly community to a relatively small but very important group of people—people whose continued good will is a vital scholarly resource. There is only one United States Congress; and its members stay around for a long time. If you blunder in any way with any of these people, you do irreparable damage to every future congressional scholar and, hence, to the scholarly dialogue. It is not like finding another city in which to study community power or another classroom in which to study political socialization.

When I first went to Washington to study the Appropriations Committee in 1959, only one out of the 50 members refused to speak with me. Less than a month before I arrived, another political scientist had walked into that member's unguarded office late in the day and tried to pressure him to give an interview. The congressman vowed he would never give an interview to a political scientist; to my knowledge, he never has; and he is now a senior member of the Appropriations Committee. Whether or not there was a cause and effect relationship here, I never forgot the incident. It has underscored a kind of Burkean view of my responsibility to other political scientists. If I leave every relationship I have with a member of Congress in as good or better repair than when I started, then I will leave Congress more, rather than less, accessible to later generations of scholars. In the interview situation, this means: Always act in an interview as if another interview with that same person were to follow soon. Psychologically, if there is no such thing as "the last interview" with a legislator, the impulse to kiss and tell is reduced. This is one way interviewers and participant observers demonstrate a commitment to science. So long as legislators are there and will grant access to political scientists, our fellow scholars can go to them and test any propositions or generalizations we present. I, therefore, do everything

I can to help the scientific enterprise by doing all I can to enhance the prospects of future interviewers.

If, in the long run, I think of myself as maintaining access for all congressional scholars, in the short run, what I am doing is maintaining access for myself. But that turns out to be a long-term endeavor. When I present my scholarly credentials to a member of Congress, I want them to reflect as good a past record as possible—in the eyes of all types of members. A lot of my personal decisions in life have been made with access problems uppermost in mind. I have not registered in a party; I have not engaged in partisan activity; I sign no political petitions; I join no political organizations or interest groups; I engage in no radio, TV, or newspaper commentary. I do not allow my name to be used for political purposes. Only once have I agreed to testify before Congress, reluctantly, on the subject of committee reorganization, a situation in which I felt I would lose future access unless I paid back members I had interviewed on that very subject. In short, I deliberately keep a low public profile—in the face of countless opportunities to do otherwise.

I do this to maximize the likelihood that *all* senators and *all* representatives and *all* their staffs will accept my professionalism and to minimize the possibility that any of them will have heard anything at all of a nonprofessional nature about me. It is altogether a very conservative approach. The point is that maintaining across-the-board access is a sine qua non of this kind of research, and it is both a long-time and a full-time effort. I keep in touch with a number of staff people as well as House members, by telephone or occasional trips to Washington. A lot of time that my fellow political scientists have to spend keeping up their statistical skills—to keep themselves in research readiness—I have to spend maintaining my access to Congress, likewise, to stay in research readiness. It is a large, yet hidden part of the research iceberg—a capital investment, an overhead cost. All this accumulated effort, for whatever it is worth, went into each travel request I made. Of course, I do not know how much, or whether, it mattered to the recipients. But it matters a lot to me: I worry about it all the time; I consider it a necessary condition for everything else I do as a political scientist.

The preceding paragraphs have been overloaded with first-person pronouns. The purpose was to accent, for political scientists unfamiliar with the research methods reported here, the indispensability of across-the-board access. There was no intention to speak for, or preach to, other political scientists engaged in field research on Congress. On the main proposition, all will agree. Problems of access are constant topics of conversation, comparison, and debate among congressional scholars. But the solutions we have arrived at are personal ones, and they vary from the deepest involvement in congressional activity to the deepest disdain for it. The personal stance I have reported here is only one variant—not better,

not worse than others, just more comfortable for me. It was reported only
to illustrate the pervasiveness, the continuousness, and the seriousness of
the access problem for people doing participant observation research. It
is especially desirable that political scientists who have never encountered
the access problem understand its fundamental importance, so that they
will not act mindlessly to undermine the research of those colleagues who
live by it.

Rapport

If access bespeaks a willingness to have me around, then *rapport*
bespeaks an added willingness to be forthcoming and frank during our
travels. Rapport refers to the state of the personal relationship—of
compatibility, of understanding, of trust—between researcher and
researched. It cannot be prescribed or taught. Sometimes it is a matter
of luck. Always, it is a challenge and a preoccupation. Because you must
constantly evaluate the quality of the data you are getting, you must,
perforce, constantly evaluate the quality of your relationship with the
person who is giving it to you. Much of what you do out in the district
is done to enhance your rapport with the people you find there. Mostly,
the way you establish good rapport is by being nice to people and trying
to see the world as they see it. You need to be patient, come on slow,
and feel your way along. Two handy hints: Go where you are driven; take
what you are given; and, when in doubt, be quiet. Rapport is less a
special talent than a special willingness to work hard—a special
commitment. And one reason it is hard work is because of the many
contexts and types of people you find yourself confronted with.

I arrived in each district with only the knowledge I had obtained from
the *Almanac of American Politics and Congressional Quarterly.* I did not do
preliminary research because I wished to come to the scene without
preconceptions—to see it as exclusively as possible through the eyes of the
member. It was a useful caution. In a district that I had selected because
of its exploding population and because I wanted to see how the
congressman coped with such instability, I found that he did not see it as
I had assumed he would. "There's been a great deal of population change
here," he volunteered.

> But beneath that surface change is a fairly stable layer of
> people who moved to the city between 1945 and 1955.
> These people have a very parochial feeling about the city.
> And they resented my opponent who had just moved
> from [a town 25 miles away]. He hadn't lived here
> before, and I think the old guard kind of resented it....
> I came to the city, started my law practice and joined the
> Lion's Club and the Methodist Church. I think those

> groups were more important to my winning my city
> council race than...volunteer workers and endorsements.
> Endorsements are very important here if you are a
> newcomer in politics.

I had the same experience in a border area district, described by political demographers as Copperhead country. The congressman talked constantly about the prevailing weather patterns from the South, but not once during my two visits did he so much as hint at any southern influence on district politics.

Early in my travels, I flew with a congressman to his district. When we got off the plane, we were met by a man who had just picked up several new suits and was delivering them to the congressman. They walked along together; I immediately concluded that the man must be a district staffer, a person of importance with whom I would be spending a good deal of time. Somewhat later, I learned that he was only a local cheerleader of some sort, and I never saw or heard of him again. But I also later learned that the new wardrobe, which seemed insignificant at the time, provided an important clue to the congressman's home style.

One month later, I flew with a second congressman to his district, whereupon we were again met at planeside by a man carrying several suits fresh from the cleaners. Recalling my earlier experience, I made a mental note that here was a typical local flunky, another spear carrier of no consequence to me. It turned out that the man was the congressman's oldest, closest, most trusted, most skilled, most knowledgeable friend.

> I trust Frank more than anyone else in the world. He's
> the guts of my operation. He knows how I want to say
> things as well as I know myself. He has insight into
> political situations that I wouldn't have.... He knows one
> hundred times more about the district than I do.

The freshly cleaned suits carried no clues to the congressman's home style. These twin experiences early in the game helped me learn to feel my way, without preconceptions, into each set of personal relationships and each new context.

When you reach the district, everything is unfamiliar. You confront a strange House member, surrounded by a totally unknown collection of people, in a new political culture, at some unknown point in an unstoppable stream of political events. One member drove 50 miles to the airport to meet me and took me to stay in his home—thus plunking me into the middle of an unfamiliar family situation. Another arranged to meet me at his campaign headquarters, came and chatted with a group of us for 15 minutes, and announced, "I'm going to go play golf with my son." Then, as an afterthought to me, "You wanna play golf?" A third had his staff tell me he would meet me at an evening meeting, then canceled the meeting—leaving me riding around a strange city at night running up a huge taxi bill. The next day he kept me waiting in his district office most of the day; and when at last he met me he said, "You should have been with us at my talk this morning. Sorry we didn't tell you about it."

Of these three situations, the most difficult is the last. In this research, getting to your respondent is the name of the game. The entire object of the trip to the district is to accompany and talk with the member—in as many contexts as possible. Yet it may not be easy. Interviewers on Capitol Hill are familiar with the secretary-gatekeeper who guards the member's office door and considers it a duty to protect the member from academic questioners. And we are familiar with the tactics—blandishment, persistence, outside intervention—for circumventing the office gatekeeper. In the district also there are gatekeepers, but they come in more complicated varieties; they may be members of the family, district staffers, campaign staffers, local politicos, and long-time personal friends. In 15 years of interviewing on Capitol Hill, I never walked into a congressman's office and found his wife there. Yet in eight district visits, I spent a great deal of my time in the company of wives—most of whom were suspicious of my motives and the effect of my activities on their husbands' careers. Several district operations were strictly "mom and pop" enterprises. Wives, like other gatekeepers, can facilitate rapport or retard it. Gaining rapport with them and with the other people around the member can be nearly as important and just as challenging as achieving it with the member.

Almost always, you are thrown into a close and necessary interaction with district gatekeepers in a way that never happens in Washington. In Washington, you may choose to spend time with a staff member; in the district, it is not a matter of choice. I was able to ride around the district alone with only 5 of the 18 members. And on only 6 of the 36 visits did I do so consistently. Nearly always, someone other than the congressman drives. Sometimes there is an entourage. The researcher rarely gets the undivided attention he gets in the congressman's Washington office. I once spent my entire three-day trip riding around attending events with a congressman, his wife, and a freshly hired district representative. The insecure district aide spent every spare minute trying to impress the congressman and ingratiate himself with the wife. He never stopped talking. I could hardly squeeze a question in edgewise. Obviously, his need for rapport was as great as mine and his claim on the congressman's time greater. I had no choice but to wait him out.

Waiting, I should note, usually paid off. The members came to feel that, as part of the bargain, they owed me something for my time and trouble. And I could count on a pang of conscience to give me what I came for. In this case, the congressman, his wife, and I went to dinner—minus the staffer—my last night in town. On the other hand, a secure and sympathetic staff member is the best insurance you can carry while in the district. In half the districts, staffers were of major importance to me, as informants, interpreters, intercessors, and friends. In two cases, the wives were extremely helpful. This is not lone ranger research. Relations with the district gatekeepers are inevitable, important, and hard to predict.

Obviously, one key to effective participant observation is to blend into each situation as unobtrusively as possible. Often, the easiest way to do this is to become an active participant. When the opportunity to participate presented itself, I snapped it up. It is an easy way to increase rapport with everyone concerned—gatekeepers as well as members. Once, for example, I arrived in a district in time to make a Friday night event, only to find the congressman had been unable to leave Washington. I called his campaign headquarters; a staffer came to pick me up and took me to headquarters to meet a collection of campaign managers and workers. They answered a few questions ("How's it going?" etc.) and then went back to their work. I sat down beside someone and started stamping and sealing a huge stack of envelopes. An hour or two later, someone asked me to help with a telephone poll, which I did. Most of the people there had no idea who I was; those who did didn't know what to do with me; and no one came to speak to me. I didn't know who they were or what each person's relationship to the congressman might be. That set of circumstances is very common. But I busied myself and, late in the evening, was shown the results of the confidential telephone poll. When I met the congressman in the morning, he greeted me with "Herr Professor, I dub thee Knight of the Telephone Poll. I hear you did yeoman service. We're going to have a campaign strategy meeting. Come on." During my ostensibly unproductive evening, I accumulated enough extra capital to be taken in as one of the group.

I have had the same results from handing out leaflets, pens, recipe books, pot holders, and shopping bags, from putting stickers on car bumpers and campaign cards under windshield wipers, and from riding around in a sound truck. Less political activities, too, proved helpful—bouncing around with the congressman on a storefront water bed, winning $19.00 from the congressman at bridge, fixing the congressman's flat tire on a mountain road, thumbing a ride when the congressman and I ran out of gas at midnight. Members can identify with you more easily if you engage in some activity—any activity—with them than they can if you just ask questions. The shared experience provides a special bond for a long time thereafter. "We missed you on election night," they often said months later, not because they really missed me but because they had come to include me in a special category—a category I had not been in when I first arrived on the scene.

71

The more immersed one becomes in the member's district activities, the more the terms of the original bargain are altered and fleshed out. Time almost always produces better rapport. Over time there are opportunities, such as the activities just recounted, to demonstrate personal adaptability. My hope was that, whereas, at the time of the initial bargain, I might have been viewed prospectively as a professorial pain in the ass, I would come to be recognized as someone who adjusts easily to the unpredictability of events, shows sensitivity to the moods of others, and needs no periodic psychological feedings. I hoped they might learn that college professors are not aloof or overbearing or self-important, that the political scientist in their midst could be ignored, patronized, laughed at, forgotten, and ordered about without being offended. In time, then, they might come to respect, if not like, a professional who would put up with all the incivilities of a political campaign to get what he wanted—one who took notes, not umbrage. Whenever working politicians can be convinced that they have found someone who wants to and does understand them and their life, they open up more than they would otherwise.

Rapport is increased, too, by the demonstration of loyalty. I took every opportunity, verbal or behavioral, to reassure them that I would not use my experience or my information to hurt them, that I was a person who could be trusted. My participation—materially trivial—was a symbolic tender of loyalty to them. I never asked people I met in the district what they thought of the member. Thus I eliminated the possibility of anyone telling the member or his associates that I was soliciting unfavorable opinions. When unfavorable evaluations of the member were offered to me, I would exit as quickly as possible. When members asked me who else I had traveled with, I willingly told them. A few names—of members they would be likely to know—invariably satisfied their curiosity. When they asked what I had learned from the others, my standard reply was "All districts are different and each member has different problems." By not saying more, I hoped to signal them that I could be trusted with their information, too. I let them know that I was not interested in their opponent's campaign. I also told them that (except in California and New York) I was only interested in one member per state, so that local political or personal conflicts would not intrude. I told them, in other words, that within the scope of their political world, I recognized a single loyalty—to them.

I did not openly evaluate their performance—offering either praise or criticism—because my posture was one of learning not judging. Requests for evaluation that might be interpretable as tests of my political intelligence were answered—as vaguely as would suffice. After his television debate with his opponent, one member asked me directly, "How did I do? A little too namby-pamby?" Answer: "If you think you are ahead, you were right not to get into charge and countercharge with him. It would only give him the publicity he needs." It was a less common kind of exchange than one might imagine.

If members found it beneficial to display me before their constituents, I allowed myself to be exploited. One member introduced me at public functions as evidence that people in other parts of the country were interested in their locality. He even introduced me in church, whereupon the minister said, as I stood amid the congregation, "Now you write good things about our congressman." Another member asked me to stay an extra day to accompany him to a college speaking engagement where he wished, I assumed, to show that group that he was at home in academic company. I agreed—as a tender of loyalty, as an extension of the bargain, and as a guarantor of our future relationships.

Only one of my group was defeated. After my postelection interview with him, I decided to get in touch with the person who defeated him, my idea being that two perspectives on the same district would be instructive. But I faced a test of my devotion to a single loyalty. Should I tell the new member that I had already traveled in the district with the defeated opponent, during the bitter election campaign? If I told him, would it contaminate all his answers? If I didn't, would I be uncomfortable acting deceitfully? I played out both possibilities at length in my mind, and finally decided that my end of the bargain required that I reveal my previous incarnation. The opportunity came before his press aid and I had left the airport. "Have you ever been here before?" "Yes, with your opponent two months ago." So far as I can tell, it did not matter. My flirtation with covert research ended.

Success in developing rapport varied. Half of them took me along when they were with their closest friends or advisors, their personal constituency. And there is not one whom I could not embarrass politically if I were to repeat remarks they made in confidence. Consider this running commentary by a member contemplating his annual appearance at a Veteran's Day observance—a member whose status as a veteran had once been essential in maintaining his reelection constituency:

> One of the things I least like to do is to sit upon the platform with my veteran buddies [but] I'll go and put on my long face.... Next year my wife will have to come to this instead of me. She doesn't believe in veterans, doesn't believe in cemeteries, and doesn't even believe in the Good Lord..... Maybe if I win by 65 percent, I won't come back here next year.

Or consider these thoughts by a member on his way to a Catholic church carnival in a district he sees as 30 percent Catholic:

> You can get more votes for fetuses in Congress right now than you can for the pork barrel. Maybe I should

73

> change my campaign button from a star to a fetus. I'm
> up there tightroping along the high wire, defusing the
> issue whenever I can..... My secret here will be to keep
> moving through the crowd—to make an elusive target. It
> won't be a leisurely stay. The odds are prohibitive
> against someone asking me about abortion. I just hope
> it isn't the man with the loudest voice in the parish.

Or consider this appraisal by one member of his respected opponent in a very close race. "He's paranoid. He is a right wing crazy; and he attracts crazy opposition like shit draws flies. People come out just to boo him." Such comments, if attributed, would not be helpful politically.

Such comments remind us, too, that the research topic of this book is no ordinary one. It involves the most sensitive of political subjects for the House member—private opinions about public issues and public people, electoral problems and electoral strategies, career ambition and career survival. I am not so naive as to believe that House members would disclose their innermost thoughts on these subjects. But their willingness to discuss them and to put themselves in some jeopardy in so doing indicates that a measure of mutual trust had been established. In answer to the question, "Compared to what?" I cannot say. More trust, probably, than is required for an ordinary Capitol Hill interview; and enough trust, probably, to justify the expenditure of time and effort put into the enterprise.

Still, rapport varied. One member, for example, remained suspicious and uncomfortable with me even after two visits to his district and a couple to his office in Washington. On my second trip to the district he and his district aide dropped me off at the hotel on a Saturday afternoon and said they'd see me "sometime Monday." I thought the treatment excessively cavalier, and my notes on the episode reflect heat and frustration:

> When they let me out at the hotel and said they'd see
> me Monday I was hopping mad. What the hell they
> thought I was going to do sitting in a hotel room from
> 4:00 Saturday till noon or so on Monday (don't you call
> us, we'll call you), I do not know. Fred is personally
> quite inconsiderate.... He never suggested I come over
> [to his place] or anything. In fact, I asked if I could go
> to his Sunday evening campaign meeting and he said,
> "They wouldn't want anyone from the outside." He also
> said he was going to some party on Sunday and said, "It
> will only be for friends." And when I got out of the car,
> he said "Don't get into trouble. But if you do, make sure
> you make it worthwhile...." To say this to me as if I had
> anything else to do but wait for him to call next Monday

was the height of insensitivity. He was treating me like some casual acquaintance he'd just met on the street someplace—not someone who had taken four days and spent several hundred dollars to come here and be with him as much as is humanly possible. Of course, he doesn't owe me one thing. But it was not what I would call friendly. I guess what really frustrates me is that I have not been able to get him to trust me. That may or may not be my fault, of course.

With regard to such an instance, observation does not stop just because participation stops. His treatment of me provided a vantage point from which I could reflect on his behavior toward others. Does he present himself to others the way he presents himself to me? Why should he be less trusting toward me than other House members are? All behavior, in other words, is grist for the observer's mill. Denied the opportunity to observe, he observes.

If insufficient rapport is one problem, then too much rapport is another. Sometimes, a professional relationship threatens to slide into a personal friendship. After all, when two people spend several days in constant personal contact—two people who share one major interest in common, politics—it is natural that a personal friendship could develop. I worried about it and tried to guard against it. I did not want them as friends—only respondents. It is impossible to be objective about one's friends. In some cases, however, it could not be stopped; if I had not acknowledged a friendship, I would have lost a respondent. If members insisted on inviting me to their homes, for example, I could not refuse. This led to occasions when I was told not too little but too much. On such occasions I deliberately pulled in my research antennae. I took no notes and tried to forget what I had heard and seen. I assumed the member was not turned on for research purposes when he or she told me about or allowed me to watch certain things—family relationships, for example. I felt it would be taking advantage of members to turn their personal revelations into data. Indeed, I felt that my refusal to get involved on such occasions was part of the bargain. I may have lost information; but I helped to keep some personal distance between us.

On one occasion, too much rapport became a nearly total impediment to research. A representative I had visited before was near the end of a difficult, bitter campaign when I arrived. And, from the moment his wife met me at the airport, I was treated as a trusted friend in a time of trouble, not as a political scientist who had come to learn about the member in his district. The member either could not or did not want to act as my teacher, as he had previously done. Again, a few excerpts from my nightly notes indicate the frustrations—and the acceptance—of too much rapport:

I'm so inside this campaign, I'm out. I find myself saying to people that I'm a friend of Carl's and I'm out here to help him out—instead of saying that I'm writing a book. I can't ask Carl questions I'd like to because it's a little like standing around someone who may be dying and asking him where it hurts the most and how bad he feels. My questions have to be carefully phrased so that they are, at least, sympathetic, and, at the most, innocent. I can't ask anything with a bite to it, anything hard, anything critical, etc. I'm treated as one of the family and I'm expected [by Carl] to act that way. As I say, I'm so far "in" that I can't be sufficiently "out" to probe. Maybe half in, half out is the best description.

I have got myself into a situation where almost no communication passes between us during the day—in contrast to my other visit when we rode all over and talked. But he is fighting for his life, and he has drawn his family around him, and I'm just "there" as a kind of friend in the background. It's even out of place to ask a question. I tried one this morning as we got to Beaver Rapids. "What kind of town is Beaver Rapids, Carl?" "Well, here it is," was his only answer.

This trip has been strange. I have been accepted and welcomed this time as a friend and not an analyst. I have been placed in a role from which I cannot extricate myself—as emotional supporter and friend. I'm introduced everywhere as "our friend Dick Fenno, from Rochester, New York"—not as a political scientist, not as an author....I have almost been anointed an intimate for this trip. When I asked Joanne [his daughter] on the way back to the house today if I shouldn't go back to the motel and leave Carl alone, she said, "No, you are good for him. He likes you and you strike just the right note with him. You are quiet when he doesn't want to talk, and you talk when he wants to. He wants people around now, and he needs people. You do it so well, you should be in public relations." She was telling me that I was needed—and I was.... [The family was busy and] he was alone, vulnerable, apprehensive, exhausted, and needed a friend. I was it. Not a political scientist. A friend.

The initial terms of our bargain were no longer recognizable. But I tried to keep my end of it as best I could, not only by acquiescing in an intensified loyalty but by keeping a blocked ear, a closed eye, and a forgetful mind to much that I observed at the time.

The Observer and the Observed

The problem of over-rapport is part of the larger problem of the relationship between the observer and the observed. It is particularly acute in participant observation research. At one level, the presence of the observer may contaminate the situation, causing the people being observed to behave differently than they otherwise might. When, for example, I allow myself to be introduced as someone writing a book about a member, those listening may view the member in a changed light. Or, if I am introduced at a strategy meeting with the comment that, "He's writing a book," the participants may pull their punches so as not to place the member in an unfavorable light. My guess is that contamination effects in these cases are pretty minor.

I have wondered, too, whether my anticipated presence in the district might cause any alterations in the scheduling. On one occasion, a member insisted on taking me to a part of the district where he had never been (during which trip he had to stop and ask some schoolchildren where we were: "I'm the congressman from Wayne and I'm looking for my district"); this unscheduled trip caused him to be late for another engagement and left him extremely irritable for the rest of the day. Because they could, and did, exclude me from events if they wished, I concluded that their schedules were probably not altered much on my account. I have also questioned whether my observation of explanatory consistency might not have been an artifact of my presence. If members were conscious of my note taking, wouldn't they have been abnormally careful not to behave like explanatory chameleons? I have no way of knowing, although I believe that I would have picked up some inconsistency somewhere along the line if such were a major behavior pattern.

Finally, the possibility of observer intrusion inheres in the very way the interviewing is done—as part of a running conversation more than as a question-and-answer session. On Capitol Hill it may be possible to nod sympathetically while listening to an interview answer, but in the district you must talk, because you are often part of a group carrying on a conversation. It is possible to have a one-sided Capitol Hill interview. It is not possible to have a one-sided three-day visit with someone. You must give as well as take; and in giving you may alter the situation you have come to observe. This is the subtlest kind of contamination. And I cannot think of a way to avoid it, except to be aware of it. Awareness will lead, usually, to saying less rather than more. It is not the object of this kind of research to gratify yourself or advance yourself personally by "making an impression" on the people you have come to observe.

On occasion, efforts to blend into the local landscape brought noteworthy success. One occurred when a very conservative member spent 10 minutes of his 25-minute press conference—before me and about eight newsmen—attacking the tax exempt status of foundations "who hire eastern egghead college professors to do social experimentation for left-wing causes." After that, the two of us went out to lunch where he talked openly about himself and his political life—to a Director of the Social Science Research Council, holding a Ford Foundation Fellowship. On another occasion, I was in a rural southern town with a congressman and the family of the local tax collector in their home. I sat quietly for an hour or so while others gossiped. Eighty-year-old Uncle Aubrey also sat quietly, in the chair next to me. At the end of the evening Sue Ann Thorp, the tax collector, asked me if I had any children and how old they were. When I said one was in his mid-twenties, everyone expressed surprise, said I wasn't old enough, feigned disbelief, and asked how come I looked so young. After a short silence, Uncle Aubrey offered his sole comment of the evening. "He takes care of hisself. He shoots and goes fishin'." His explanation settled the matter for everyone present. For a tennis player and a skier, it was the highlight of seven years of research.

The larger danger in the relationship of observer and observed is what anthropologists call "going native"—becoming so close to your respondents, so immersed in their world and so dependent on this close relationship that you lose all intellectual distance and scholarly objectivity. Thus does the observer of Congress, having lost any critical capacity, become an apologist for the members and the institution. This is a problem to which there is no completely satisfactory solution. I recognize it, I worry about it, and I have tried to cope with it—again, mainly by keeping relationships professional. The effort has had only partial success

The primary bulwark of one's professionalism in these matters is a natural one. Political scientists live within a scholarly community; and so long as they identify with that community, they will remain outsiders in the world they go to observe. After my earliest set of four district visits, university colleagues asked me how things had gone. And I can recall telling them that things had gone well, but it was "good to be home"—that only by going out of the intellectual community could one realize how much more at home he was there than in any of the districts. Everywhere I went I had been an outsider; and I had felt like an outsider. The four districts visited definitely ranked differently on my personal at-homeness index; but compared to the university, all ranked far behind. However comfortable I may have felt, I was uncomfortable compared to the way I felt within the scholarly community. It was a contrast that continued to the last. That contrast in feeling is, perhaps, the academic's surest barrier against going native.

I had gone to the district thinking that Robert Merton's classification of "local" and "cosmopolitan" (among others, of course) might help me differentiate among House members. I left the districts thinking that the distinction was useful, not for differentiating among members, but for differentiating between members as a group and the political scientists who study them, between the observed and the observer. Compared to academics, nearly all House members are locals. Compared to a university, most congressional districts are less cosmopolitan. Members tend to be rooted in the values and the institutional life of local communities. They belong; they know where they belong; and it is the very strength of our representative institution that they do. The academic, on the other hand, is likely to be less locally rooted, more mobile, more attached to free-floating intellectual communities, an outsider in any context beyond the scholarly one. And most so, perhaps, in a local space-and-place bounded context like a congressional district. In terms of going native, the marginality of the academic to almost all native contexts is a natural asset. In terms of understanding the working politician with local ties, however, it complicates the task of participant observation.

As a complement to this natural professional marginality, I have found it personally helpful to remain marginal to the congressman's world in Washington. I have never lived there. I have never spent more than three weeks at a stretch there. Between 1968 and 1977, with the exception of a single two-week stay, I never spent more than three days in Washington at any time. When I am there I do not socialize with members or their families; nor do I become entangled in the alliances of the Washington community. It has been my habit to go there, collect data, and return to Rochester to puzzle over what I have found and to work out my conceptual and analytical structures within the scholarly community. Because other academics find it equally beneficial to spend much time—to live—in Washington, I suspect my hit-and-run relationship with Capitol Hill is a personal idiosyncrasy. (It is also a matter of what one has chosen to study in Washington.) I am sure, however, that the practice has raised the odds against going native in my particular case. And I mention it only in that respect.

Out in the districts, as noted earlier, some members became friends. But they remained business friends rather than personal friends, social friends, or family friends. It is the best measure of our personal relationship that not more than two of the 18 know anything but the most superficial things about me personally. I never volunteered; most of them never asked; and that is the way I like it. (It was always reassuring to return to a district after two years and be introduced by a member with whom I had developed fairly good rapport as a professor from "Syracuse University" or from "Fordham.") A clear failure in my efforts to preserve a business relationship, however, is the fact that I could not bring myself to be indifferent to their electoral success. *I wanted them all to win.* Nothing I did, however, had the slightest effect on whether or not they did. In one bizarre set of circumstances, however, I became emotionally involved in the campaign of my oldest and closest congressional friend; I had no effect on the electoral outcome, but I became an intimate for the duration of the campaign; and in the process I abandoned all social science activity. Luckily, I had nearly completed my research in that district.

A final, less soluble part of the observer-observed, going native problem is that in doing the things that must be done to maintain desirable levels of access and rapport, the participant observer can slowly lose the ability and the willingness to criticize. Some loss of objectivity comes inevitably, as increased contact brings sympathy, and sympathy in its turn dulls the edge of criticism. Some blurring of intellectual distance is produced, too, by the pleasures of participant observation research. The problem is that across-the-board access and continued rapport require a sympathetic understanding on the part of the observer. By the same token, they probably also require that highly opinionated and unflattering commentary be avoided. I have felt, for example, that my access might be adversely affected if I jumped heavily into the debates on congressional reform—which are, after all, debates among partisans within Congress. (If they are not, they are trivial and meaningless exercises, and it doesn't matter to anyone which side a political scientist might be on.) This conservative posture, taken in the interests of access, provokes scholarly criticism for being insufficiently sensitive to congressional change, too wedded to the status quo—in short, a "Congress lover." I think the thrust of such criticism is correct. Political scientists who are less encumbered than I by a felt need to protect across-the-board access and rapport will have to produce the most thoroughgoing critical work on Congress.

I also think this kind of work is necessary if others are to provide informed, relevant criticism. My books have not been uncritical. When members engaged in the same behavior—running against Congress, for example—serious criticism has been levied. But, of course, blanket criticism is not as likely to affect access as the criticism of individuals would. In that respect, some of my work has been less biting and critical than it might have been. Still, I know that some of my judgments—however mild—will bother individual members, because their view of themselves is bound to be more flattering than mine. (This is largely, I think, because my judgments—that they are issue-oriented, or hard working, or personable, or creative, or whatever—are inevitably comparative and, hence, relative to their colleagues. Their self-estimates, on the other hand, cannot be made relative to what their colleagues do at home, since they have no opportunity to observe. Hence, they judge themselves more in comparison to other politicians in their home context—most of whom are less successful than they.) By protecting their anonymity, I have tried to shield them from any criticism from their colleagues and from people at home who might use attributed material against them.

If there were any way that I could have "named names" in my work, without destroying my access and without jeopardizing the access of future political scientists, I would have done so. It would have given my book's ideas a much wider national audience than it ever got, attached as they were, antiseptically, to Representatives A, B, C. But it could not be done. Political science friends of mine know the names of some of the House members with whom I have traveled. Doubtless, some will play games matching names with letters. But they cannot expect any helpful signals from this quarter.

Data

When I am with each House member, I do a lot of what I call "hanging around." That is, a lot of watching, listening, and talking, a lot of sitting, standing, and riding, some participation, and a lot of questioning—all for the purpose of collecting data. A three-day trip would produce 25 to 35 pages of notes, typed and double-spaced. How good, then, are the results? How reliable and valid are the data collected in this manner? In the end, each reader will have to make some judgments. I can only describe how it was done, what the problems were, and how I tried to hedge against them.

The data. I use in the book are my notes; note taking is central to the work. I do not use a tape recorder. In the unresolved dispute among elite interviewers, I continue to stand with those who prefer not to use one. I am most comfortable interviewing politicians in a relaxed, conversational manner, without intrusion of mechanical devices that have to be started, reloaded, and stopped. To some degree, doubtless, this reflects the defense of an established style against the unknown—against the fear that whatever effect it might have on the interviewee, a tape recorder would cramp my style as an interviewer. To some degree, it reflects an unwillingness to risk the costs involved in a test that might confirm my fears and result in as much as a single bungled interview.

But, more than just taste or conservatism, my reservations about a tape recorder relate to its possible adverse effect on the interview—in light of the purpose and uses to which I put the interviews. In exploratory research, the emphasis is on discovering relationships and on generating ideas about them. And the interviews are most useful when the conversation is most frank and most spontaneous. I would gladly trade many a whole interview for one personal reflection that provides me with a new way of looking at things, for one insightful formulation that is rooted in personal experience, or for one particularly apt and pungent commentary. If insight and nuance and example and free association are to be encouraged, it is my belief that one's chances of getting a "better" interview are increased when no tape recorder is used and person-to-person rapport is the only reliance.

To be sure, most House members will talk with a tape recorder present. And the fact that they will talk for the record is good enough for some research purposes. Where data collection is to be followed by quantification, where content analysis and coding will be necessary, the need for reportorial accuracy is probably the paramount consideration. In such cases, a tape recorder may be mandatory. Such is also the case where journalists seek comment for attribution. But where you want to maximize the likelihood of qualitatively interesting comments, the tape recorder can only be inhibitory.

Every congressman has a fairly stylized set of comments that he is willing to make for the record. Some will do so more willingly and volubly than others. But all of them—or so I believe, and this is probably the crucial assumption—have a second, qualitatively different level of off-the-record commentary they could engage in. That is the level I want to reach: the level of commentary for private consumption that lies between a level for public consumption and a level for no consumption. If there are members who give all they have to give on tape, they will do so without tape. For the others—and a key assumption is that there are many "others"—my belief is that the only chance to get a nonroutine, nonreflexive interview is to converse casually, pursuing targets of opportunity without the presence of a recording instrument other than myself. If worst comes to worst, they can always deny what they have said in person; on tape they leave themselves no room for escape. I believe they are not unaware of the difference.

Contrasting viewpoints on recording methods will be resolved only by the different tastes and assumptions of researchers and by the different purposes of their research. It is impossible to prove that an interview obtained in one way was not as "good" as the interview that would have resulted from the use of a different technique. I have simply made an educated guess for my kind of research. I would only add that whatever the interview technique, the proper attitude toward the results should be skepticism, leading to reevaluation and, wherever possible, cross-checking. We should not be beguiled by the mere fact that politicians will talk to us. They are professional talkers—professional "presenters" as we have said. They have a big personal investment to protect, and they have learned how to protect it against all outsiders, whether we come carrying our tape recorders or not.

For home district research, the tape recorder issue is largely moot. Most of the time it would be impossible to use, because so much of the interviewing is conducted on the run, because it is utterly impossible to predict when or under what conditions the member will be responsive to questioning, and because the best results often come in isolated moments of informality and spontaneity. There is no one "best time" for this kind of interview; there are many such times, most of them brief and unexpected. The closest thing to a generalization might be that morning proved the least promising; the member was usually preoccupied with organizing and rehearsing the day's activities.

My technique was to carry a pocket-sized notebook and to record, as nearly as my powers of recall would permit, verbatim quotations. I recorded whenever I had a chance during the day. Sometimes I made brief jottings—of key phrases, for example—to remind me of things I did not want to forget; sometimes I recorded a few of the most salient comments completely and immediately. Just how much I could get into the notebook during the day was in the lap of the gods. During the first day or two when I was working hard at rapport, I often sacrificed data to rapport by not taking notes unless I was totally alone. I wanted to appear relaxed, to blend into the picture, and to encourage the members to relax by not giving them the feeling that I was recording everything they said. When I felt I had achieved decent rapport, I would very conspicuously take notes, to remind them of our professional relationship and to reassure them that I was really working on a book. I began to do this routinely because, once we got to know each other, some members would ask, "Aren't you going to take any notes? How do you remember all this?"

The answer to the "how do you remember" question is simply that you train yourself to do so. You learn to switch on and off as subjects of interest come and go and to spend the time when you are switched off rehearsing and imprinting the items you wish to remember. The most revealing comments are unforgettable. In any event, my technique was to take mental notes, transcribe them briefly when I got the chance during the day, and then to spend two, three, or four hours in the evening recording everything I could remember about the day's activities and about the member's comments. I did this in the same notebook. Besides writing the data, I wrote down my reactions to what I had seen and heard, all the additional questions that had come to mind, all the analytical ideas that had occurred to me, illuminating comparisons between this member and other members—a running commentary on the data. I reread my notes whenever I got the chance to jog my memory and add items I had forgotten.

The major organizing principle of the notes was chronological. It aided me both in my recall and in my reflections if I recreated the day chronologically when debriefing myself at night. I found, too, that I could remember the context in which statements were made or actions taken if I thought about the day's activities in sequence. The minor organizing principle of the notes was a running speculation on "what makes this particular member tick." This involved an effort to find some consistency in his or her action and comments. I would describe for myself a tentative pattern, then worry over behaviors that did not seem to fit the pattern and entertain tentative revisions that would accommodate the unexplained patterns. Much of this theorizing has been excluded from the book—for instance, my private speculations about "personality" characteristics. But I tried to understand "the whole member" in some depth as a precondition for any attempt to offer generalizations about all members. The more I satisfied myself that I understood one member's perceptual and behavioral patterns, the more confidently I could add one more case to my generalizing base. In some cases, the effort produced no consistent pattern and, hence, uncertainty on my part. But the effort always helped me to remember and organize what I had observed.

In trying to make sense out of each member's activity, I found it particularly helpful to compare him or her with other members. Practically, this meant comparing two members—occasionally three—with whom I traveled consecutively. While one experience was still very fresh, I would think about a given member's home style by comparing it in detail with that of the last member and vice versa. Table A illustrates the frequency with which such stimulative bunchings occurred. These "constant comparisons" helped to highlight what was special about each member while also building a tentative set of generalizations about their similarities. These comparisons were an additional aid to memory and to reflection. But in my notes they always had a limited, two- or three-member scope and never of a comprehensive, eighteen-member scope.

The discussion of note taking illuminates a basic characteristic of participant observation research. Data collection and data analysis do not proceed in linear progression. They proceed simultaneously. Participant observation is not like survey research, in which you make up a permanent set of questions, put your questionnaire "into the field," wait for the data to come in, and then proceed to do "data analysis." In participant observation research, data analysis accompanies data collection, and the questionnaire that goes into the field may change in the course of the research. The differences should not be exaggerated; but the ones that exist stem from the different strengths of the two kinds of research—the one more confirmatory, the other more exploratory.

This bare-bones description of my data collection methods is sufficient to indicate numerous problems. But whatever problems inhere in the technique are compounded by the conditions under which this kind of research is done. First, it is physically tiring. When people ask me what I have learned, my first answer is that politicians have incredible stamina and that, surely, when we think of recruitment we should take this basic factor of sheer human energy into account. At its worst, it means getting up at 5:30 for the factory gates and going to bed after the last evening meeting at night. For them, there may be sleep; for the observer, there are two or three hours of note taking left— to bed at 2:00 a.m. and up again at 6:30. There is no time to leave the scene to pull yourself together; you just keep going. After three or four or five days of this, I was worn out—but they kept right on.

Worse than the physical fatigue, however, is the mental weariness that results from this kind of research. For the member, there is a lot of routine to what he or she does at home. Besides, there is a lot at stake. Even more, it is, for members, an ego trip and they are buoyed up by being on center stage. Standing in line for a drink at a realtor's open house, I said to a bone-weary member (who had to be dragged to the party), "A drink will pick you up." He smiles, "No, the people will. As soon as I get on stage, I'll begin to dance a little." All this makes it easier for him to keep up the mental as well as the physical pace. For the observer, however, nothing is routine or ego-gratifying. Everything is strange, yet everything must be accommodated to—new people, new culture, new challenges. The sheer overload of information—faces, places, events, statistics, history, all different from those of the last district—is overwhelming. Yet they must be quickly assimilated, retained, and fed back to the people around you in familiar usages, at appropriate times.

Moreover, the benefits of all this are not so certain for the observer as they are for the member. How do I know whether I'll get anything useful? I am 2,000 miles from home and $600 poorer, and how do I know I'll have any decent rapport with these people? If I know the member is going someplace but no one has suggested that I go along, should I speak up and run the risk of seeming too pushy or sit back and run the risk of not being asked to go? Should I ask my question now or should I wait? I carried around a shotgun loaded with questions, but had to feel my way into a situation where it seemed propitious to squeeze the trigger. Once, when I held back on my questions for two days, the member got a cold and a sore throat on the third. Once, flying in a small Cessna, I had just begun to ask some questions when the pilot suddenly turned the controls over to the congressman. Sometimes, with a staffer driving the car, a trip across the district can be an ideal time for asking questions. But what do you do when you find that one member likes to sleep on such trips, another likes to listen to tapes, and another likes to play the harmonica? Do you try to get a conversation going or do you wait? I waited, realizing that they might be trying to defend themselves against my questions—to find a private, quiet time for themselves before plunging in again. But I couldn't relax. If the member awakened, turned off the tapes, or put down the harmonica, I had to have my questions lined up in order of priority and ready to fire.

The uncertainty and the anxiety associated with this kind of adventure are great. In a 45-minute interview on Capitol Hill you typically have the undivided attention to the congressman, and you keep firing questions until he (or you) terminates the interview. It is not a matter of discretion whether or not to ask a question. It is part of the bargain that, for the duration of the interview, you will ask and he will answer. But in the district, the bargain is that you are allowed to tag along and observe whatever they do and ask appropriate questions at appropriate times. Each time you ask a question, however, it is a matter of tact, of judgment. Frequently, you are asking the member to change the focus of his attention from something else to your questions. (I always carried a detailed map of the district with me, and found that taking it out and asking "Where are we now?" was one fairly easy way to shift focus.) You must constantly assess the situation for its appropriateness, its ripeness. On Capitol Hill, you do not care about the congressman's state of readiness, how fatigued he is, where he has been, where he is going, what is worrying him, whether now will be "better" than later. You walk in at the appointed time, sit down, and ask your questions, and hope to fit questions most naturally into the flow of conversation and events.

These matters of discretion are anxiety producing. If I blow one interview on Capitol Hill, it's no big loss—on to the next office! Anyway, it probably wasn't my fault. But if I blow one in the district, it costs a lot, and it probably *was* my fault. In sum, my behavior is a good deal more consequential in the less routinized, more complicated, and totally unpredictable district setting than it is on Capitol Hill.

There is a lot of time, too, to brood about such matters. Despite the frenzy of activity all around, the role of the observer is very solitary. You are marginal—deliberately so—to every group you are with. Rarely will anyone come up to make you feel at home—at a dinner, a cocktail party, a celebration, a meeting. They are playing their games. The House member is playing with them. The more the member is interacting person-to-person with others, the less the participant observer can either participate or observe. You must move away from the member as he goes about the business of handshaking, greeting, and talking with his constituents. Although no one in this gathering of total strangers is paying the slightest attention to you, you can give no indication of being anything less than completely comfortable, of not thoroughly enjoying yourself. It's a little bit like the basketball player's ability to "move without the ball." It is lonesome duty; anyone who tends toward paranoia should not volunteer. This is not a complaint. Like the House members running for reelection, my first comment is "I must be crazy to do this," and my second comment is "I can't think of anything I'd rather do." But—given the physical and mental fatigue—I found I could not visit more than two districts in succession or last more than seven or eight days on the road, however much more economical and intellectually stimulating longer trips might have been.

These working conditions only exacerbate the problems of data collection. What are these problems? One is that because so much of my note taking is done after the event, a subtle reconstruction of the event or comment can take place in the interim. Another is that I will have selectively perceived and simply have missed a lot that was said or happened. This danger is made worse by the oceans of talk that wash over the observer in such a visit. To try to record, as I did, as much as I could, whether or not it interested me or made sense to me at the time was only a partial solution. Such words and events tend always to be "second thoughts," recorded after the apparent highlights. Another problem is that I will have failed to record the context in which a comment was made, thus endowing it with greater generality than it was intended to have. Finally, because I was not the same person when I began in 1970 as I was when I finished in 1977, changes in my own interests and abilities may have made generalizing across time hazardous. These defects in the human recording instrument are made more serious by physical and mental weariness. And I would never claim that my notes do not suffer from all these limitations.

Data so collected produced any number of worries. One is the matter of accuracy. Did I get what he said—the right words, the right order, the complete thought? Did I observe what he did correctly or fully? One is the matter of validity. Am I using each example of words or of actions to illustrate something appropriate to the meaning the member gave it? Another is the matter of reliability. Have I arrived at a fair, durable representation of each member's thoughts and acts in making my generalizations about his or her perceptions or behavior?

I have tried to cope with these problems and worries. Mainly, I have done so by making two trips to as many districts as possible (14) and by supplementing these trips with an interview (11 times) in Washington. My hope is that, by repeated as well as prolonged soakings in the district and by the kind of cross-checking that a Washington interview will provide, I will increase my chances of getting it right, using it right, and portraying it right. I know that my own confidence in the data and in my use of it increases exponentially when I can add a second set of observations to the first.

The more you observe, the more practice you get in matters such as note taking and recall; and the more practice you get, the more accurate you become. Oftentimes, the same thing will be said twice during a visit; and the second account is more nearly verbatim because you need only fill in the blanks. Sometimes, the same perception is articulated on both trips and cross-checking increases accuracy. During the Washington interviews, I took close to verbatim notes and tape recorded immediately thereafter, thus giving me another check. The hiatus between visits—usually at least a year—allowed me to accumulate a fresh list of questions, some repeats, and some new ones. I could reformulate my earlier hunches, and puzzlements, as to home style patterns or as to "what makes this member tick." When you see or hear the same thing repeated more than once after a period of years, you feel more certain how to interpret what you see. If, for example, you visit a district and see the member do nothing except give speeches (or never give a speech) you wonder whether this represents stylistic preference or a contextual coincidence. When you return for a later stay and see the identical pattern, you feel more secure about making a stylistic generalization based on observation. Or, if you make very different observations on successive occasions, you may be able to interpret this in terms of a consistent developmental pattern or as some idiosyncratic activity related to a very specific context.

Generalizations made by working politicians tend to be based on recent events and are, on that account, always suspect. It is not a matter of deceit. It is just that politicians live pragmatically from immediate problem to immediate problem and have neither the time nor the incentive to generalize beyond what happened yesterday, or last week, or, maybe, last month. The observer needs methods, therefore, for determining whether a given comment—seemingly important—is to be interpreted as a considered generalization or as an artifact of a specific context. When you hear the same thing repeated on more than one occasion—especially on occasions widely separated in time—you can have more confidence that it is a usable generalization.

Conversely, if a comparison of the notes from two visits shows a marked change in emphasis, you may be able to see the relevance of context. For example, when I asked a congressman in a heavily Jewish district, in 1970, whether any single vote cast in Congress could defeat him, he answered with unusual confidence, "I can't think of any vote that would defeat me. Not a single one. Even if I voted against arms for Israel, I could prepare a defense and say that there weren't enough *arms* for Israel." In 1976, when I returned to the district, he spontaneously volunteered the comment, "If I voted against aid to Israel...that would be it! If I did something absurd like that and voted counter to a massive opinion in my district, I would lose." The generalizations he made in the two cases were important. But they have to be seen as contextually produced—by the upbeat confidence resulting from the Six-Day War, which prevailed during my first visit, and by the shaky uncertainty following the Yom Kippur War, which prevailed during my second visit.

In short, two sets of observations are better than one—much better. It is not just that you can compare notes taken across time and contexts. It is also that rapport invariably is better during the second visit than the first, and, hence, you learn more and learn better. Here, for example, is a congressman discussing his reelection and career goals. On the first trip, his only comment on the subject was:

> Eighty or 90 percent of all members of Congress are
> always looking ahead to the next election. They pick
> each other's brains on the subject all the time. I don't

care what they say, that's on their minds. Just like a
business with a profit and loss statement, the politician
looks at the next election as his test. There are some
independent cusses down there. They know what's right
for the world and they go ahead and do it. But most of
them aren't like that.

On the second trip, we had not been together an hour before he launched
into a soliloquy, part of which went:

I don't know what I'm doing in this business or why I
ever got into it. The family situation is terrible. I just
spent 10 days in the district. Dottie and the kids were
here for the first three days and then they drove back to
Maryland to start school. I went back Wednesday, went
to the office and then had to go to a dinner for the life
underwriters groups. A congressman from our state has
to go. If you don't, they won't speak to you again. Then
I got home late that night. The next day I had to go to
a breakfast and another cocktail party to see some people
from the district who were in town. So I got home late
again. That was yesterday and here I am back in the
district again for five days. I'm a yo-yo.... You work so
hard to get it and when you get it you wonder what you
did it for. It's like joining a fraternity—I worried so
much about it, but when I got to be president of the
House, it didn't matter anymore. It's so competitive. I
like that. And I like the excitement. But you spend so
much time and effort—for what? I'll tell you—to get
reelected. I'll be more frank with you than I would be
with most people. We spend all of our time running for
reelection.... I guess I told you before, I'm not going to
grow old in Washington. I may run for the Senate if
things work out. If I win, okay; if I don't win, okay. I'll
be happy to go back home. If I do win, I'll make a
solemn promise to myself that it won't be for long. But
I would love to have six years and not have to run all the
time. I'd say, "I don't care what happens, I'm not going
to spend all my time running for reelection."

During my first trip, this same member had kept me waiting in a
parking lot while he went inside to talk strategy with some intimates. On
the second trip, he took me to his strategy meeting.

One characteristic of the interview data is that it is nonstandardized
and, hence, not quantifiable. Questions are tailored to particular
individuals and are posed in dissimilar contexts—not to mention in
scrambled orderings. Nonstandardization is, indeed, essential to getting

and keeping rapport. And the result is that the material is not easily coded or described in terms of frequencies. It was never my intention to quantify this material; it was not collected with quantification in mind; and I do not think it would be methodologically sound to quantify it retrospectively. But I have, of course, supplemented my field work with two kinds of quantifiable data: first, data on numbers of trips home and allocation of staff resources, and, second, data taken from the appointment books of members. The first body of data, anyone can collect. But data from private appointment books could not be had by anyone lacking good rapport with the member. In addition, several members gave me precise rankings of the importance and the comfortableness of their various activities at the end of my visit. That, too, is not something that would be done for the casual observer. Thus, maybe this type of research, although not in itself quantitative, can open up avenues of research that are.

The book's data are, however, mostly nonquantifiable. That is the reason so much of it has been presented in the form of quotations. Some are lengthy and complicated. Altogether they may become tedious. But they need to be struggled with, like any other kind of data. Data analysis, of course, will have to be done by making nonnumerical assessments of meaning, appropriateness, consistency, context, and importance. Readers should not think of the quotations and anecdotes herein as any less worthy of serious examination than other kinds of data. They are, of course, primarily discovery data and should be viewed in this light. Because "data analysis" is often assumed to mean only the statistical manipulation of numerical data, it should be noted that participant observation is likely to produce data of a different sort and require different modes of data analysis. In the final accounting, we ought to ask the same serious question we would ask of any set of data: Have they served the purpose for which they are gathered?

One way to rephrase this question about the adequacy of the data is: Are your data any better than, or any different from, what you would have gotten by interviewing on Capitol Hill? The answer is, I think: for the particular purposes of the book "better," and in a more general sense "different." The data are better because there are some questions I would not have known enough to ask had I not put myself in the district—all the questions about home style, for example. Had I simply taken some perceptual questions to Capitol Hill, the *Home Style* book would have ended with Chapter One. Even then, it would not have been as informed a chapter. Questions about perceptions (of each group or area as we visited them, for instance) can be formulated and answered more knowledgeably at the point where the member is actually engaged in perceiving.

Passing a number of pickup trucks on the road, one congressman in a heterogeneous district commented, "This is Wallace country. You can tell a Wallacite because he has a pickup truck, a hound dog, and a gun. He'll give you his dog and his pickup truck, but he won't give up his gun." The next day, spotting several pickup trucks as we entered the parking lot of a VFW hall, he said, "I'd love to get the pickup truck vote, but I never do." A congressman trying to win support from lower-middle-class voters despite his strong civil rights record revealed a relevant view of these constituents as we drove along a city street: "We're a very artsy community here. A few years ago, they built a theatre in the round across the park there. And do you know what it turned into after two years? A wrestling hall. I guess that tells you something about the state of culture in the district." During the evening's rehash of another member's day's activities, someone mentioned the morning hour of handshaking, howdying, and hijinks with 20 people in a small country store. The congressman turned to me and said simply, "Dick, those are the people who elect me." In each case, the circumstances elicited spontaneous perceptual statements; and, because I had observed what the congressman was talking about, I understood better what he meant.

Through repeated and prolonged observation in the districts I also discovered patterns of behavior that I would not have known about otherwise—the lawlike tendency of House members to run for Congress by running against Congress, for example. In these several respects, I think the data are "better" than they might otherwise have been.

Equally, however, the data are simply different. I did not learn many things I did not know before. But I came to know through experience things I had known only intellectually; I got "a feel" for things. It is one thing to know that a district is "agricultural" and that "the farmers are worried about the drought"; it is another thing to find yourself unable to place campaign cards under car windshield wipers that have been glued to the windshield by inches of caked dust. It is one thing to know that a district is "inner city" and that "the people there feel powerless"; but it is another thing to scrape your car axle on cratered, unpaved streets in the heart of one of American's largest cities. It is one thing to consult a map and note that one of the two districts you are about to visit is "small" an that the other is "large"; it is another thing to sit in a strategy meeting in the first district where it is concluded that three billboards will capture all the traffic in the district, and then go to the second district to spend one whole day driving to a town of 2,500 people.

When these things happen, you begin to *weight* factors differently in your thinking, giving more weight to things experienced than you otherwise might have. Because these experiences are selective, it may be dangerous to pay special attention to them. On the other hand, it may be possible to better understand the congressman's own weighting when you have experienced his concerns at first hand. And, no matter what else it accomplishes, a better "feel" for a district helps offset the natural disadvantages—discussed earlier—that university-oriented academics face in understanding locally-oriented politicians.

Just as you gather different data about the districts, so do you come to form a different picture of politicians. Again, the point is that you do not learn anything new so much as you place different emphasis on old knowledge. Intellectually, I knew that politicians required physical stamina; having flogged myself around 18 districts with them, I now think physical attributes are more important to political success than I had previously believed. The second attribute of politicians that has been highlighted by these visits is their sheer competitiveness. It is not, at this stage, so much a matter of a driving ambition to be a congressman. They have achieved that ambition; and there are other things they can do to make a living. But they do not want to lose. They may have learned how to lose gracefully; but they *hate* to lose. We know they want to win; but they seem now to me more driven by a determination not to lose. They are, above all, tough competitors.

A third attribute that looms somewhat larger to me now is the politician's ability to keep from taking himself too seriously. It is something an outsider has less opportunity to observe on Capitol Hill, where each House member seems, at least, to be a king or queen in his or her empire—isolated from everyday life, fawned over by a staff, pampered by Capitol Hill employees, sought after by all manner of supplicants. House members may, of course, be able to take a wry view of this existence. But it may be easier to do so in the district, where they are more likely to be reminded of their ordinariness. In any case, they display a marked ability to break the tension of competition at home by indulging in humor or whimsy, to keep some private perspective on their public selves.

> *Congressman*: I dreamt last night that I was defeated. No fooling, I really did. And do you know what bothered me most? The House gym! My wife said to me, "You're a distinguished person; you'll get a job, don't worry." I said, "Yes, I know; but where will I find a gym like that?"

> *Wife*: A man called and asked you to call him back no matter how late you get home tonight.
> *Daughter*: Your opponent says you're only interested in big business, and not the little folks.
> *Congressman*: We'll I'll find out who he is first. If he's big business, I'll talk to him. If he's little folk, I won't.

Staffer: What are you going to say at the next meeting?
Congressman: I'm going to ask somebody to give me a haircut. Or, I could walk in and hang from the chandelier. No, I guess I'll walk in, undress, and say, "Any questions?"

There may be no generalizations possible about politicians. But when people ask me what they are like, I now stress stamina, competitiveness, and a stabilizing perspective on themselves. I would not have stressed the same things after my Capitol Hill experience.

Because my research was undertaken partly to acquire the vantage point of "the country," one might wonder whether I developed any "feel for the country." Only this, that any claim by anybody to have a feel for the whole country would be preposterous. For ill or good, no one can comprehend the United States. Watching 18 people will tell anyone that much. Perhaps, of course, looking at "the country" through the eyes of members of Congress is not the best way to comprehend it. But if House members, whose business it is to know only a small segment, express so much uncertain knowledge of their segment, it is not immediately clear who is better equipped to comprehend the whole. Only institutionally, not individually, can it be done. To travel outside Washington is to experience and, hence, to weight more heavily the diversity of the country. That weighting, in turn, emphasizes the enormity of the institutional task. One returns to Capitol Hill asking of our representative institution not, "How come you accomplish so little?" but, "How come you accomplish anything at all?"

Evaluation

Despite what seems to be a monumentally uneconomical method of collecting data, I think the results *are* different from what I would have gotten in Washington. Whether the data are "different enough" or "better" depends on what you want them for. And so we return to the most serious question about data: Are they adequate for our purpose?

It is a final characteristic of participant observation research that this judgment must be made by two groups—political scientists and the people being observed. It matters little to the machinist's wife in Dayton what Scammon and Wattenberg's book says. It matters even less to Scammon and Wattenberg what she thinks about their book. But it matters enormously to me what House members (and the people around them) will think of my study. If they say, "That's how it is; that's the way we think," then I have captured something of their world. And I will have passed what I consider the first test. For if they cannot recognize their world in what I have written, I will have failed in the most elementary way. I will have soaked and poked in their world and not been able to see what they see there. Not that they would or could *generalize* about it the way I have. That is my job. But I want them to recognize their perspectives and their perceptions in my observations.

Members of Congress do not normally "rush to judgment" on academic works—not in my experience. Many of them will not even acknowledge receipt of academic work, let alone read or comment on them. A few members, however, and more staff people do read what political scientists write and do pass judgment. Some journalists, too, perform a similar function. I have had no experience with the reactions of political people in the district—whose judgment will be important in this case. On Capitol Hill, although most people remain oblivious to what we do, nonetheless, the judgment of the few percolates around provides an ultimate check on our scholarship. On the whole, the Capitol Hill community—again, I have no experience with people in the districts—is predisposed, if not eager, to demolish political science scholarship for its lack of contact with real world politics. Favorable judgments are all the more important, therefore, because they are hard to come by.

Among political scientists, community control will operate to produce judgments on this research. For them, several questions will be raised. Does the description ring true, in accordance with whatever experience political scientists have had with the people and the activities covered in the book? Vast numbers of political scientists have had firsthand experience in the world about which I have written; their sense of my descriptive accuracy and relevance, therefore, will also be necessary to any favorable evaluation of the research. Political scientists will ask, further, whether the description sheds any light on problems they have been worrying about. Does the study say anything that other political scientists—whether or not they use participant observation—might think worth incorporating into their thinking? Will political scientists find questions posed here interesting enough to pick up and pursue—by participant observation or any other method?

In sum, political scientists will ask whether the work seems accurate and, if so, whether it is worth remembering. They will not answer yes to these questions unless they think the research has been conducted with some care and unless they think the data are adequate to the project's exploratory purpose. If the data are judged sufficiently "different" or "better" to produce some yes answers, then the data are—for all their obvious problems—good enough for me. In the end, whatever research methods we use, we keep each other honest.

4

What's He Like? What's She Like?
What Are They Like?*

It is the special characteristic of the House Speaker—and the source of his influence—that he touches more phases of the political process than anyone else in the legislative branch. Observing the speaker provides a special opportunity to see that larger system through his eyes. We might use the subject of congressional leadership as a window on the wider world of American politics. Or, more narrowly, we might use the perspective of *congressional leadership* to look at *congressional politics*. I want to address this narrower relationship. I want to do it as a political scientist addressing other political scientists. My main point is simply that if we look at congressional leadership in a particular way, it might make us want to know more about the ordinary member of Congress. And political scientists, I want to suggest, might profitably expend more effort learning about the ordinary members of Congress. A focus on leaders, in short, might end up producing a focus on followers.

Individual Legislators and Their Leaders

This is not a paradox. All of social science tells us that leadership involves a relationship between leader and follower—that one cannot be

---

*Presented at the Thomas P. O'Neil Symposium on Congress, Boston College, January 30, 1981. Published by permission of Transaction Publishers from *The U.S. Congress*, Dennis Hale, Editor. Copyright (c) 1983 by Transaction Publishers.

understood without the other. And all of our studies of congressional leadership point us in the same direction. Studies by Robert Peabody and Nelson W. Polsby, of the way in which House and Senate leaders get elected, tell us that the leaders of Congress are chosen by the ordinary members of the Congress, for reasons known only to those members themselves—and with a minimum of outside influence. In most congressional dramas, everybody in the political system can play. In picking congressional leaders, only the followers can play. To most outsiders, leadership contests are nonevents; inside Congress, they are matters of great intensity—fought "eyeball to eyeball" as one Republican leadership candidate described them.

When the ordinary senator or representative chooses among prospective leaders, each member asks himself or herself this question: "What can he do for me?" or "What will my life be like with him as a leader?" The followers think of leadership, therefore, in terms of a personal, individual, one-to-one relationship between the leader and each of them. And in so doing, the followers set the basic conditions under which their leaders must function. As one veteran senator put it, "For a leader's job...you want a fellow who will treat you fairly. You wonder how a person will conduct himself in the job with particular reference to *you*." An experienced House member defined leadership the same way. "You only want two things in a leader," he said, "first, someone who will see you and, second, [someone who will] understand your problems." Such is the highly personalized follower's view of congressional leadership.

Not surprisingly, when leaders talk about their job, they stress the same one-to-one relationship with their followers. "There's no mystery about being Senate leader," said Lyndon Johnson. "You've got to be interested in the *other fellow's* problems." Leaders know that is how they get and keep their job. Speaker Carl Albert said, "The main element in my climb to the leadership is the fact that I've heard more speeches and called more people by their first name. I've always been fascinated by [the members].... There are so many variances and eccentricities." An ordinary member who helped start Albert on his leadership climb—from whip to majority leader to speaker—agreed: "He's done so many things for so many people, they trust him.... They think, 'Here's a man I can talk to.' When the members go about picking a leader, they want *personal service*." A biographer of Senator Robert Byrd explained his promotion from majority whip to majority leader similarly: "If there was one factor above all others that marked his service as whip, it was that he drove himself from early morning to late evening to meet the *personal needs of individual senators*."

Congressional leaders often move up the leadership ladder from a subordinate position to a higher one—as Byrd did, or as Albert did or as Robert Michel did. The backlog of personal trust and personal credits they have built up with individual members is taken as a warrant of similar assistance in the future. Speaker O'Neill advanced up the leadership ladder in the same manner—from whip, to majority leader, to speaker. He was chosen whip in large part because individual House Democrats felt he would be accessible to them. *Congressional Quarterly* headlined his selection, "New Democratic Whip: Friends In All Factions." When he was later elected majority leader, the man who challenged him and then withdrew said in the caucus, "Tip, I can tell you something that nobody else in this room can. You haven't got an enemy in the place." When he was elected speaker he told the freshman Democrats, "My policy will be an open door policy. I am easy to talk to." At each rung of the ladder, O'Neill built up enough credits with enough individual members to earn a promotion. At the top of the ladder as speaker, he continued to devote a great deal of time to doing what he had always done—help his followers, one by one.

"When Tip walks onto the floor," said Representative Joe Moakley, "it's like throwing a piece of sugar at ants. The guys line up to talk to him." And the speaker said, "I get everybody who has a problem. It's like a priest hearing confessions. You can't say no." O'Neill spent an estimated one in four weekends on the road, visiting in the home districts of from 30-40 House members each year. What ordinary members want from their leaders is a personal relationship and personal service. And that is what they get. They get it in Washington and they get it back home.

This personal relationship is not a one-way street. While the leaders are doing what their followers most want them to do, they are at the same time learning what they most need to *know* in order to lead. Sam Rayburn's assistant, D. B. Hardeman, attributed Rayburn's success as speaker primarily to his "intelligence," because, said Hardeman, "he applied this intelligence to knowing the member and his district, sometimes even better than the member himself." In Lyndon Johnson's words, "A good leader should...know the problems of each individual state and the temperament of each individual senator." A good leader, says Robert Byrd, "should understand the problems of individual members within their own respective constituencies. He should know his colleagues, their personalities, their interests." House majority leader Jim Wright travelled to the constituencies of 83 House Democrats during his first year and a half in office. But he learned about his followers while he served them. "It's fatiguing at times but richly rewarding," said Wright of his travels. "It helps me in my job, knowing the concerns and aspirations of members. It also helps me to elicit their support for the Democratic program."

Leaders must know their followers as individuals because at some point leadership involves the act of persuasion. Leaders must persuade followers to do something or not to do something—to support or not to support a certain procedure, to vote or not to vote for a certain amendment, or to oppose or not to oppose a certain bill. Persuasion in the Congress is a person-to-person process, done most effectively by someone who knows each individual he is trying to persuade. That is, by a leader who has the kind of knowledge about each follower that Wright and Hardeman and Johnson and Byrd talked about. The personal, one-to-one relationship that followers expect of their leaders is the same kind of relationship that leaders must seek out if they are to be effective.

So, personal service and personal persuasion are two sides of the same coin for the leader. They require the same concern about individual followers. Either way, from the leader's perspective, the key question about each follower is: "What are his or her problems?" "What does he or she want?" Or to put it most generally, "What's he or she like?" Congressional leaders must answer this question for each senator and representative in order to get their job, in order to keep their job, and in order to do their job. This question—the "what's he like" or the "what's she like" question—is a crucial question for congressional leaders. I think it should become more of a political scientist's question, too.

When I first went to Washington to study Congress in the early 1960s, the people I talked to on Capitol Hill invariably placed great emphasis on this kind of question—on what they called "the human equation" or "the personalities involved." In 1961, Majority leader John McCormack replied to my questions about assigning members to committees with this typical comment:

> Of course, personality enters in. Like any group of fellas on the corner, you have different personalities. Some members are more popular than others. Some of the members are brilliant, but they are lazy. Others are not so brilliant, but they develop what they have and they work hard. Some men are eloquent speakers, but they don't have that "it" to make a speech. Others don't speak so well but they've got the courage to go down and say what they feel.... Some members are there for years and years and no one ever knows they are there. But we known they are there, [that] they are doing their job here—all different. We take all these things into consideration.

Other Capitol Hill people were more critical. "The trouble with you political scientists," they would say, "is that you don't understand that all these personalities are different." My reaction was to brush aside all such comments—descriptive or critical. I wrote them off as the naturally protective posture of people trying to carve out a part of the process that outsiders, like political scientists, could not hope to penetrate. Even more, I tended to feel that the knowledge they withheld from me was unimportant in the development of theories about congressional behavior. Information about particular individuals, I felt, was grist for the mill of journalists, whose short run, episodic focus made them more interested in such matters—more interested in "anecdotes" or, as political scientists are wont to say "mere anecdotes"—than in generalizations.

I am no longer convinced of my wisdom in such matters. Why? For one thing, I now believe that my Capitol Hill respondents were telling me something of theoretical importance. They were telling me that the desires and the goals and the abilities of individual members and the relationships of trust, respect, and obligation they establish with one another—leader to follower for example—can be important in legislative politics. It might be difficult (as surely it is) to acquire usable knowledge about individual legislators, but the result might well bring an enhanced understanding of why people do what they do in the legislature. So, the "what's he like—what's she like" question might be more important than I had thought. And, therefore, answers to that question might lead to generalizations more consequential than I had imagined—generalizations about "what are *they* like." For, that question—*what are they like*—is ultimately the political scientist's question. And I came to believe that our answers to it might be better if we devoted more time looking at individual members.

For another thing, it is a simple fact that some of the most stimulating work on Congress has been produced by journalists—by people who have wrestled quite unabashedly with the "what's he like" question. And often in anecdotal form. I think of Elizabeth Drew's book on Senator John Culver, Bernard Asbell's book on Senator Edmund Muskie, and Jimmy Breslin's book about Speaker Thomas O'Neill. Drew describes the personal aspect of Culver's effectiveness; Asbell describes the priority Muskie places on achieving personal credibility among his colleagues; Breslin describes the speaker's personal approach to consensus building in the House. Political scientists need to know about these things.

Willy nilly, therefore, we will feed off these studies, just as we have fed off perceptive journalistic studies in the past. Students of Congress should remember that it was a journalist, William White, who set the agenda for 25 years of political science scholarship on the Senate with his book, *Citadel*, published in 1956. The echoes of White's ideas on "what are they like" dominate even the most recent political science books on the Senate—Ross Baker's *Friends and Foes in the U.S. Senate*, and Michael Foley's *The New Senate*. We should acknowledge our reliance on perceptive journalists. But at the same time we might ask ourselves: Why should we leave the journalists in charge of the "what's he like" question—and, hence, in charge of the "what are they like" question? Why, indeed, should we leave them in charge of anecdotes? As Raymond

Wolfinger has wisely observed, "The plural of anecdote is data." We might have better data if we collect it ourselves.

Of course, political scientists have not totally neglected the "what's he like" question. Indeed, another reason for entertaining that question lies in the success enjoyed by some political scientists who have done so. For example, David Mayhew's discussion of the advertising, credit claiming, and position-taking behavior of House members was stimulated by his service in a congressman's office. Morris Fiorina's essay on the importance of constituency service was stimulated by his interviews in two congressional districts. In both cases, the authors began with the "what's he like" question and moved to "what are they like" generalizations. They, and others like them, moved the study of Congress forward by making and pressing such generalizations.

But there is reason to believe that political scientists have just scratched the surface—if only because we have devoted so little time and energy to the "what's he like—what's she like" question. Up to now, our major "what are they like" generalization states that members of the House and Senate want to get reelected. That is, for example, the driving generalization behind the Mayhew and Fiorina studies. Certainly the reelection goal is an important one for our legislators. And no answer to the "what are they like" question would be complete without the notion that most of them want to keep their jobs. But I doubt that is all there is to it. Members are probably more complicated than that. If Speaker O'Neill knew about each House member only that he or she wanted to get reelected, would the speaker have known enough to keep his job? Or enough to do his job? I doubt it.

Which leads me to a final reason for looking at individual members. When Speaker O'Neill was asked the "what are they like" question, he had his generalization about them. It was that the members were *independent*—significantly more independent than they used to be. "You have such a wave of independence," he said. Or, "They're all independent now." Or, "Years ago, most of them came from their local legislatures. They'd have been seasoned. But now 50 percent of them have never been in public office before. There's a tremendous independence." Or, "They have no sense of party discipline. They run more as individuals." Or, "They're younger. They're better educated. We have more graduates and Rhodes scholars, more doctorates, more master's degrees—people who came into the field of politics as a challenge with the idea that they wanted change—extremely independent." This was the speaker's constant theme. Robert Byrd echoed the idea for senators. "The emergence of 'the individual' has been a kind of phenomenon," he said.

If legislators are strikingly more independent now—more individualistic—then congressional leaders will have to spend more time than they ever did getting to know the ordinary members—one by one.

The individual member cannot so easily be subsumed in a party, or a committee, or a bloc, or a delegation as once was the case. Recent elections, furthermore, have produced increased turnover among the memberships of both chambers. Sixty-one percent of today's House members have served six years or less. Sixty-two percent of today's senators have served six years or less. Therefore, as Barbara Sinclair has observed, at the very time it becomes more important for the leaders to know the individual members well, it has become more difficult for the leaders to do so. The "what's he like—what's she like" question has become increasingly important *and* increasingly problematical for congressional leaders. So political scientists have yet another reason for spending some time on it.

Knowledge about individual members helps congressional leaders do their job—influencing behavior. More knowledge about individual members might help the political scientists do their job—analyzing behavior. At present, we are more knowledgeable about legislators in the aggregate than we are about the building blocks that make up these aggregates. Our graduate students are required to learn statistics—the better to manipulate aggregates. But they are not required to talk to politicians—the better to understand aggregates. Would our analyses be improved if more of us actually met our politicians? We can't be sure. Still, I should like to tease a few more into trying.

A Citizen Legislator

In the 1970s I got to know 18 members of the House pretty well—by travelling with them in their districts and by talking with them in Washington. In December of 1980, one of those 18 left Congress. He left of his own volition, at the age of 50 and after only eight years of service. He had no electoral worries. Like most of the 435 members of the House, he remained unknown to the American public outside his district. Nor was he a person of any special influence in the House. He was, in that sense, a perfectly ordinary member of Congress. Because I know him and because he has left public life, I can ask the "what's he like" question more easily of him than of other members. So, I shall. His decision to retire, to return to his home town, and to resume the private practice of law also gives the question a little extra bite, since his desire to get reelected will not get us very far in answering the question.

His leaving drew one bit of national notice. Otis Pike, a former House colleague and a Democrat devoted a syndicated column to the retiring member, a Republican. Wrote Pike:

> On the evening of February 6 in the House of Representatives, [he] gave an important speech. It is about war. It should be required reading. [He] is an

intellectual, but not an orator. There are better speakers in the House, but none who have more to say. He writes his own speeches and speaks his own mind. It is a superb mind.... He is, also, retiring this year and the Congress and the nation will be poorer for it. No one in America heard the speech and almost no one outside the Fourth District of Colorado has heard of Jim Johnson.

So, "what's he like," Jim Johnson, Republican of Colorado? Like 534 others—complicated. He is a former marine jet pilot who, when asked to speak at a Marine Corps dinner, recited from memory Rudyard Kipling's antiwar poem about "Tommy Atkins." He is a man who, in 1976, could be seen throwing paper napkins at his friends during Colorado State University's raunchy sports banquet and who, in 1980, wanted very much to be the new president of Colorado State University. He is a cofounder of a successful water-toothbrush business, Aquatec, who sits on the Board of Trustees of a Presbyterian seminary. He is a cocktail party charmer who reads each of Shakespeare's histories 3 or 4 times a year.

He was, according to a man who should know, the best theologian in the House of Representatives. "Imagine," says House Chaplain James David Ford. "Here I am a Lutheran pastor. I have spent nine years in school studying the Bible. I've travelled all over the world and talked scripture with ministers of all faiths. And I have to come here to the House of Representatives to find someone who knows as much about scripture as I do. That's Jim Johnson." And, he adds, "People don't believe it, because he uses such salty language, and because he jokes all the time." I have listened to him swap funny stories with people all over Colorado; I have never heard him talk about his religion. As I say, complicated.

Politically speaking, Jim Johnson was nothing if not independent—the very prototype of the House member described by Speaker O'Neill and, thus, very much a congressman of his time. He first ran for Congress in 1966 as a strong opponent of the Viet Nam War—in a Colorado district that, said one veteran reporter—"has more lobster pots than it has doves." He lost that year; but he ran again, as an antiwar candidate in 1972 and won. The public mood had changed. But Johnson's persistently dovish views put him permanently at odds with some members of his party in Colorado. Three times the Republican right wing fielded a candidate against him—twice in the primary, once in the general. When he got to Washington in 1973, his first activity was to organize against further U.S. military involvement in Cambodia—a stand that did not endear him to some members of his party in Washington. Johnson had strong convictions on the matter of war and peace. At home and in Washington, his attitude was the same. As he stated it when we first met in 1974 "I don't have any great desire to impose my moral beliefs on other people. But I'm not going to vote with the majority just because they believe something, if I don't believe in it, too. I have no great love for this job. If I lose next time, that's fine. If I win that's fine too." He had run to make his voice heard on matters of public policy about which he felt strongly, and he intended to do just that. "I have spoken up more on the floor and gotten into more debates than almost any other freshman," he said at the end of his first term. "These are issues of life and death importance to the country, and I'm not going to sit there and keep still." As I say, independent.

In 1976 he was appointed the Select Committee on Intelligence to investigate the work of the CIA. Coming close, as it did, to his strongest policy interests, he regarded that assignment as "the most interesting and important thing I've ever done in my life." Johnson broke with his fellow Republicans on that Committee in favoring publication of the committee's report—a move opposed by the Republican administration. And it was then that his leader, John Rhodes, had to cope with the independence of his follower. "Rhodes asked me to back down," he recalls. "I knew I was playing the Democrats game. But I couldn't change my views. It was the time that my views and Rhodes' views diverged, and it was the end of my career within the Republican party." When he made his speech in favor of publishing the report, "I got a standing ovation from the Democratic side. On our side, everybody was silent." When the permanent Committee on Intelligence was set up in 1977, he sought membership on it. But he did not get it.

Jim Johnson was not only independent of party but independent of major interests, as well. Colorado's Fourth District is vast and diverse. It is the district of James Michener's book *Centennial*. Covering the top one-third of the state, it is, says Johnson, "four different districts." As he describes them, "The far east is mostly concerned with agriculture, the foothills of the mountains on the east are suburban; the mountain area on the continental divide is mostly tourist, a resort area and small mountain towns that are ranching-oriented and the far west is agriculture and mineral development" (coal and oil shale). Michener writes that his town, Centennial, stood "at the spot where a man could look eastward and catch the full power of the prairie and westward to see the rockies. The history of the town would be a record of the way it responded to the impossible task of conciliating the demands of the mountains with the requirements of the prairie."

Johnson's home town of Fort Collins stands near that spot, and Johnson's job was precisely that of conciliating these diverse interests—sometimes competing with, sometimes oblivious to one another. The nature of these interests put him in the middle of some of the toughest issues of the 1970s—energy, environment, natural resources.

When asked by an editor on the front range "Is it possible for you to represent the western slope and the eastern slope at the same time?" He answered simply, "I don't know. But that's the job I've got." Later, he said:

> You do the best you can as a whole. I try not to worry about one group. I try to think of what they want but not their reactions in terms of my career. I'll go home and try to explain it. If you're not fearful about the job, you are more relaxed in it, more confident. I don't know what it would be like to worry about every vote. Some try to calculate the effect on some group. I don't. It's a wasted mental process. It takes your energy away from the question, "Is this bill reasonable?"

Johnson's reasonability test produced a very checkered, almost inexplicable voting record in Congress. The Colorado Democratic Party chairman called him "the greatest enigma in Colorado politics.... We don't understand his voting record, the papers don't understand his voting record. The people don't understand his voting record."

When I asked him who his strongest supporters were, he said "Just personal friends. And the reason is I've never been an ideologue. My voting record is not 100 percent for anything. I think labor has some points. I think the ACA (Americans for Constitutional Action, a conservative group) has some points. My ACA rating was 67 percent. The ADA (Americans for Democratic Action, a liberal group) gave me the highest rating of any Republican in the state." His distance from any large interest is reflected by the relatively modest amounts of money he spent on his campaigns, $51,000 to capture the seat in 1972, then $53,000, $65,000, and $92,000 to hold it. In every case, he spent less than his opponent—less than half as much in the year he won the seat and $70,000 less the last time he ran. If there was any interest toward which he leaned, it was the farmers. "The farmers are not numerous," he said, "but they are the most important part of the state's economy." For that reason, he went on the Agriculture Committee. But neither the Farm Bureau nor the National Farmer's Union had supported him when he won in 1972. As I say, independent.

A distinctive attitude toward the job breaks through in his reflections. It is that serving in Congress is no big deal. And this attitude underwrites his independence on the job. On the way to a retirement party thrown by his friends in the House, I asked him "What do you tell your colleagues when they ask about your retirement?" "That I'm tired of it and I want to go home," he said. "Is that taken as a sign of strength or as a sign of weakness," I asked. "It's not taken any way at all," he said. "It's taken as an event of no great moment." Back home in 1974 when asked by interviewers why people should vote for him, he would reply "I turn that question back to the voters. If you like my record and accomplishments, vote for me. If you don't, don't." On to the next question.

He worked hard to get the job; but he had no sense that, for the benefit of others or of himself, it was important that he keep the job. He appears to have been "hooked" by it only once—after he lost in 1966. "Once you have run for Congress and lost you never get over it," he said. His wife added, "It was the only thing he had ever failed at in his life." His 1972 success provided the necessary detoxification. And his retirement announcement was characteristically matter of fact. "I never intended to make a permanent career in Washington," he wrote, "and it is time to come home to stay." As I say, no big deal.

We should think of Jim Johnson as a citizen legislator. He is a man who got agitated about a public problem, went to Washington to see what he could do about it, did what he felt he could do about it, and then returned home to resume his career. From beginning to end, issues of war and peace were the ones that Johnson cared most about. When he decided he could do nothing about these matters, he decided to leave. "The Congress does what the public wants them to do," he said in 1980.

> Right now, the people want a military buildup—the Carter doctrine, the MX missile. You can feel it coming—rolling, rolling—and there is no way I can make a difference on that issue. It was the war that was the motivating factor for my getting into politics. For a while, we could do something, because the public was opposed to the war. But everything has changed now. There's nothing I can do to advance the things I believe in—the important things.

When President Carter announced his Mid-East Doctrine in his State of the Union message, Johnson got up quietly and walked out. But he did not publicize the act. A month later he gave a short speech about it—the one Otis Pike wrote about. "I can make speeches about the important things I believe in, and a few people will sit there and listen," he said. "They are polite. But their attitude is, 'There goes Johnson. He's a nut on that subject. We'll let him talk but we won't pay any attention.' Everybody is allowed to be a nut on some subject. But that's all there is to it. You don't get anything accomplished." Persuasion, he says, does not occur on the House floor.

Implicit in his decision to leave Congress rather than to continue such speechmaking is a distaste for publicity seeking and self-advertisement. Whoever heard Jim Johnson's voice in the congressional peacemongering chorus? Otis Pike, maybe. A Colorado reporter wrote about his leaving:

> Congress is losing one of its endangered species—a serious legislator who couldn't care less about media coverage. [He] seldom sends out press releases, has only

held one press conference in seven years, and doesn't
believe in wasting the time of the House with lengthy
speeches.

He wanted to accomplish things for his cause, but not through
personal publicity. And in that sense, he was not a congressman of his
time. He was asked to run for the Senate. He thinks he could have won.
Indeed, he has all the qualifications for a Wayne Morse type role in the
Senate. Except the interest. "I don't think I could accomplish any more
in the Senate than in the House—not with the public thinking the way it
is. Congress just isn't the place for me." The decision to leave Capitol
Hill seems final. But, he said later, "If I saw a war starting up some place,
I would have no compunction about running again, to make my voice
heard." As I say, a citizen politician.

Johnson's sense of frustration in matters of war and peace was not
matched where his committee work—on the Agriculture and Interior
Committees—was involved. "I've learned how to work the legislative
process, and I enjoy it" he said in 1976. He worked well with the
Democratic majority, smoothing the way for committee consensus and
accumulating a number of concrete accomplishments. For example, "The
Democrats let me put my name on the Historic Trails Bill. It's not a
great thing. But I'm proud of it." In talking about his decision to leave
he commented in 1980,

It's not a matter of my being unable to get anything
done. It's not sour grapes. I have managed more
legislation on the House floor than the whole of my
delegation combined. I have my name on more pieces
of legislation than any of them. I don't say it isn't
worthwhile or that it isn't fun. It is. And I could go
on doing that for a long time. But that's not enough.

From his strategic location on two constituency-oriented committees
he produced legislative benefits for the Fourth Congressional district—the
designation of three wilderness areas, money for local governments from
mineral leases, money for water recycling projects, money for the removal
of uranium mill tailings. But he hewed to the distinction between the
important things and the little things; and he ultimately judged his
accomplishments on the important things. It might be correct to say that
he had unrealistic expectations in this respect. That may be a problem
with citizen legislators. But by all conventional standards, Jim Johnson
was an effective member of the minority party in the House.

At home, too, he was an effective politician. He increased his
election margin steadily from 51 percent in 1972 to 62 percent in 1978.
He assumed the district could be his for a long time. No one disagreed.
The district has had only four congressmen since it was created in 1914.
Its very diversity makes it both hard to capture and easy to defend. By

the time I watched him campaign, in 1974 and 1976, he had developed a relaxed, low key, comfortable relationship with the bulk of his constituents—as befits a secure defender. "What I like to do," he said, "is to get in the car with Mac McGraw [a district representative] and go around to the small towns talking with people like the banker. The banker is central to everything that goes on in town. You can learn more by talking to him for an hour than you can any other way. And there's that sense of community, too, that I feel comfortable with." The comment reflects a central concern for the *quality* of his constituency relations.

Invariably, he did less than his aggressive, more quantitatively oriented campaign staff would program for him. In 1974, he spent an hour talking with a pharmacist in the town of Craig while a couple of campaign aides sputtered in the cafe next door. Not energetic enough, they said. Too interested in the few on Main Street and not interested enough in the many in front of Safeway, they said. "It doesn't fit my temperament to shake hands without stopping to talk with each person," Johnson commented later. "Then I feel like I can understand them and they understand me. Like that pharmacist in Craig. He disagreed with me on a lot of things and gave me a hard time. But after we talked, he said, 'You've got a tough job.'"

Two years later, we had a replay—with the candidate showing the same disinclination to squeeze every vote out of the situation. On an afternoon when he was scheduled to work the business district in Estes Park, he spent the entire time talking to an art gallery proprietor and an artist next door. "He's a lousy campaigner" exclaimed the staffer afterwards. But on the ride home, Johnson again commented on the quality of his constituency relations:

> The attitude I have is that there isn't a grown man or woman alive that isn't worth listening to sometime. People acquire knowledge, skills, and insight in various ways. And there isn't anyone who doesn't have some ideas worth listening to. Some of the Birchers I give short shrift to. But even there I spent two hours talking to five of them over in Ault the other day. And later one of them came back smiling to give me more information. My constituents are tolerant with me because I am tolerant with them. People might not be for me because of some issue, but there isn't any animosity toward me anywhere in this district.

What Johnson valued most about his relationships at home was the "sense of community" about which he spoke—the comfortable feeling that he and his constituents shared enough by way of experience and outlook to talk to one another, to understand one another, and to respect one another. "I need that sense of community," he said. But he could not achieve it everywhere. When he left the small towns of the mountains, the western slope, and the eastern prairie and the small cities of the front range and went to the mushrooming suburbs nearest Denver, he lost all sense of community. Over on the western slope, in Meeker, in 1974, he had talked about the suburban segment of his district:

> I hardly ever campaign there. How can you? It's not a community. The people who work there don't live there. They have no shopping centers where everybody shops. They have no rotary clubs or groups like that. It's just a bunch of houses. I went to a picnic there once and they said, "You haven't been here before." I know it. I know I don't represent the Denver suburbs very well.

Without that sense of community and without community institutions to plug into, he felt lost. When we rode into those same suburbs two years later, he exclaimed:

> Now we're coming to the area that gives me the heebie jeebies. I don't know how to campaign here. So mostly we don't. We come and walk around with our thumb in our ear.... The Chamber of Commerce sent out 700 invitations to a meeting and 17 came. We announced that we would be at one of their senior citizen community centers and two people showed up. We went door to door and nobody was home—just dogs. There are no community leaders to talk with. We put a district office here, but I don't know that it does any good.... They think their Representative is Pat Schroeder. It's the most miserable son of a bitchin place I've ever known.

His inability to identify with this 15 percent of his district only highlights his strong sense of identification with the other 85 percent. His attitude toward most of the district was not fear, but pride. He went out of his way to take me to visit with the grand old man of his district, the man who had defeated him in 1966—Wayne Aspinall. "You get a proprietary interest in your district," he said. "Aspinall had it, too." In 1976, he pointed out to me the man he hoped would succeed him in Congress—State Senator Hank Brown. Johnson nurtured Brown's candidacy by making him his campaign manager in 1976. Brown was elected to Congress in 1980. As I say, a sense of community.

I have dwelled on this qualitative dimension of Johnson's constituency relations for two reasons. For one thing, it was the quality of this relationship that allowed him to act independently in Washington. He could be a dove in a hawkish district, and he could produce a checkered voting record without worrying about the reaction at home. "There's no reason to fear your constituents," he said in 1976. "There's no reason to look over your shoulder. Cast every vote as you see it and then go home and explain it. People are tolerant. They ask me to explain. They don't say "you're a ding dong." I watched him do a lot of explaining at home. His explanations on both sides of the Rockies and in the middle, were devoid of demagoguery. They were as matter of fact as he was himself; and they were educative. To complaining cattlemen on the western slope, he said that the dairymen on the eastern slope were worse off. To people in favor of the West Divide Reclamation Project, he said that the people who worried about flooding beautiful country had a point. He told people on the western slope that the Denver Water board had reasonable people on it; and on the eastern slope he told people it was unfair for them to keep water from the western slope farmers who needed it when Denver had no need for it now. He regularly told one group that another group in the district had a different viewpoint—trying always to engender that essential tolerance, constituent to constituent as well as constituent to congressman.

"I think educating your constituency is the most important job we have," he said. On my experience, Johnson did a lot—more than most. In return, he was allowed great freedom of maneuver inside the House. When a newsman asked him to spell out the "guidelines" he used in balancing the wishes of his constituency against his conscience, he answered:

> I don't have a checklist. Are you a flyer? Well, flyers have a checklist they go through.... But lawyers don't think in those terms. It's foreign to our experience. I always think people who ask that question don't understand legislation. Legislation is a kind of art. A legislature is a human institution. You have to know what the House is like, what is futile, what is possible. You have to understand when to compromise and on what—or, when not to compromise at all.

The sense of community he established in Colorado undergirded both his legislative freedom and his legislative effectiveness in Washington.

The value Johnson places on that sense of community helps, finally, to explain his decision to retire. For there was a life style element to that decision. "The lifestyle [in Washington] is not compatible with mine," he told a reporter in Colorado in 1976. "I don't like living where I'm not a part of a community, working with the church, the boy scouts, the Chamber of Commerce. These bring remuneration to you as an individual. You don't have that in Congress." In 1980 he returned to that theme. "I'll be going back to a rut. But it has a lot of the advantages as well as the disadvantages of a rut. I'll be able to participate in the church, participate in the community. It will be a more wholesome life." Wholesome for him as an individual. Not only did Washington deny him a sense of community but at the same time, it denied him a sense of challenge. Life in Congress did not allow him to engage all his abilities. "I felt I was degenerating," he said of his life on Capitol Hill.

> I was wasting too much time. You don't get out of here till 7:00 and so you go back to your office and drink with your buddies. You drink too much. Traffic is bad, so you wait and you don't get home till 9:00. What kind of family life is that? Most of your time is spent listening to bullshit and jollying. That's fun. But it's not productive work. You aren't using your faculties to the fullest. You degenerate.

"It's a little terrifying," he said, thinking of his return to the law. "You don't have the confidence you did when you first got out of law school. But if you succeed—and I always have—you will have a sense of accomplishing productive work. You will work all day every day and go home at night." When Johnson said about his accomplishments in Congress, "It's not enough," he was thinking of personal fulfillment as well as policy achievement. As I said at the outset, complicated.

So what are we to make of this look at one ordinary member of Congress? Not much. With one case it is possible to prove everything or nothing. Maybe Jim Johnson is unique. But maybe if we looked at more individual members we would find he is not. We won't know until we try. And I am only arguing that we try. We might find that he falls into a class or several classes of members about whom we could or should make more general statements—"what are they like" instead of "what is he like?" At this point we can only guess what these classes of legislators might be. Let me suggest a few.

First, Jim Johnson might belong to a class of members who hold very strong views about certain public policies and whose goals as legislators involve the pursuit of their favored policies. Hence, their behavior as members of Congress can be explained to a large degree by understanding their policy views and the intensity with which they hold to those views. At the moment, our political science research seems to be underplaying such people.

Second, granted the independence of present-day legislators, Johnson might belong to a class of members whose independence in Washington is underwritten by the quality of his or her constituency relations at home. If so, we can only understand a member's behavior in Congress by knowing more about the qualitative dimensions of relationships back home. Legislative leaders who travel to the districts of their followers probably know all about these connections. But political scientists might want to collect and codify such matters with our interests in mind.

Third, Johnson might belong to a class of citizen legislators, who retain strong ties to their home area and who are either dubious about or opposed to making a career in Congress. If there is such a group of legislators, we might study their effect on the institution. Senator Henry Bellmon, retiring from the Senate after two terms, suggested in his farewell speech last month that congressional performance would be improved if we had more citizen legislators and fewer professional legislators. A debate over the limitation on legislative terms seems destined to go on for a while. Political scientists might want to contribute to it by examining the current citizen legislator class—if such there is.

Fourth, Johnson may belong to a class of legislators who find the job insufficiently challenging. What they want most is to be pushed to the fullest use of their individual talents and abilities—and they find that they are not. So, they lose interest. A newspaperman-friend of Johnson's said to me, "I think it's a problem for the country when people of his caliber lose interest. I think that's what happened to Jim. He lost interest." Should we be worried when a Jim Johnson loses interest and goes home? Should we be worried when a legislator loses interest and does not go home? Political scientists might want to find out how much legislative behavior is affected by members' attitudes toward work and accomplishment, challenge, and fulfillment.

Finally, Jim Johnson may belong to a class of legislators who deserve better from the great American public than they get. At a time when Congress is not held in very high esteem and at a time when so much scandal-fueled street talk concludes that "they are all crooks," an examination of the reality—by classes of legislators—might lead to a different judgment. Perhaps there is a class of members who are deserving of public confidence. How large a class might that be? Is there anything special about Jim Johnson? Or is he what we have called him, "ordinary." Who knows? There are 535 legislators out there. Political scientists have not spent much time looking at any one of them.

5

Observation, Context, and Sequence[*]

All students of politics are, perforce, students of politicians. Whether we place them near the center or at the periphery of our work, we cannot avoid thinking about those people who, in any society, pursue public careers, make public decisions, and enmesh themselves in public values. There are, of course, many ways to study politicians. I wish to address one of them: observation. By observation, I mean following politicians around and talking with them as they go about their work. My experience in observing some United States senators relates most directly to people with an interest in American legislative politics. But I should like to engage all those interested in what politicians do and why. The main question I wish to pose is, What, if any, value can the close personal observation of politicians bring to our studies of politics? A secondary question is, Should we, as a discipline, encourage more of it?

The observation to which I refer is, for lack of a better term, interactive observation. It is not like looking through a one-way glass at someone on the other side. You watch, you accompany, and you talk with the people you are studying. Much of what you see, therefore, is dictated by what they do and say. If something is important to them, it becomes important to you. Their view of the world is as important as your view

[*]Reprinted from the *American Political Science Review*, Vol. 80, No. 1, March 1986.

of that world. You impose some research questions on them; they impose some research questions on you. That interaction has its costs—most notably in a considerable loss of control over the research process. It also has benefits. It brings you especially close to your data. You watch it being generated and you collect it at the source. It is not received data. Furthermore, these data—the perceptions, the interpretations, and the behavior of working politicians—are data that bring you close to serious political activity. This immediate proximity to data about serious political activity produces sensitivities and perspectives that give observation some "value added"—almost certainly for students of American legislative politics, and quite possibly for all political scientists who think about politicians.

We are not talking here about a theory of politics. We are talking about a mode of research. But it is a mode of research that can—potentially at least—inform, enrich, and guide theories of politics. Its potential may be greater for some bodies of theory than for others. The very activity of observing politicians carries with it a bias in favor of individual-level theorizing. It is individuals you are watching and it is generalizations about individuals that become the building blocks of your analysis. My own view begins with the idea that politicians are both goal-seeking and situation-interpreting individuals. It proceeds to the idea that politicians act on the basis of what they want to accomplish in their world, and on the basis of how they interpret what they see in that world. It moves from there to the idea that we can gain valuable knowledge of their actions, perceptions, and interpretations by trying to see their world as they see it. And hence to observation. I shall make a minimum claim for it—that it brings value added to individual-level analysis. But I hope that others might explore its further reaches for possible contributions to more macro-level theorizing.

Context and Sequence

There are two large lessons to be drawn from observation. Each flows directly from a basic condition of observation as a research mode. First, in order to observe politicians, you must leave the place where you live and work, where routines and people are familiar, and go to some other place where you intrude—more or less—upon the lives, the work, and the routines of less familiar people. In order to observe politicians, you must operate in an unfamiliar context. And that basic condition drives you, inevitably, to a sharpened appreciation of *context* as a variable in your analysis.

The relevance of context becomes increasingly evident as you move from the observation of one politician to the observation of another. You are driven to ask, in each new encounter, Who is this person I'm with? What is he or she trying to accomplish? What is the situation in which he finds himself? How do he and his situation differ from that of other people I have observed? The object of your attention is "this person." But unless you are engaged in the study of individual psyches—as most of us are not—the unit of analysis is always "this person in this situation." You face an individual who is pursuing certain goals, holding certain personal attitudes and values, carrying a residue of personal experience. But you also face an individual who is perceiving, interpreting, and acting in a complex set of circumstances. And you cannot know what you want to know about that individual until you have knowledge of these "circumstances," or this "situation," or, this "context." By knowledge, I mean to include what you learn by looking at the context yourself and what you learn by seeing the context through the eyes of the individual politician. Observation involves interviewing; but it involves much more than interviewing.

There are two master contexts in which all legislative politicians work—home and the capital city. They can be observed in both places. I began by observing some United States senators at home. That experience conveys, overwhelmingly, the importance of context.

During my first two days with a senator from a large state, he held consecutive meetings with a conference of black ministers, a conservative citizens' group, representatives of two dozen national PACs, officials of the statewide Catholic Conference, a group of Jewish community leaders, the political operatives of the State Education Association, and officers of the Teamsters Union. Three weeks later, I spent my first full day with a small-state senator, driving across vast farmlands for a series of leisurely visits with groups of citizens in three small-town cafes. I saw the meetings in the large state as impassioned importunings, with various groups interviewing a prospective advocate for their cause. I saw the meetings in the small state as easygoing exchanges, with each group reassuring itself that the visitor was "one of us."

The contextual contrast I saw fit with each senator's own perceptions and interpretations. The large-state senator sees himself working in a contentious context, characterized by a great diversity of organized and insistent groups. He calls his state "a microcosm of the United States." Cultivating it, he says, presents "the same problem that a lawyer with a general practice has, of handling many clients without a specialty. It's the problem of dealing with hundreds, even thousands of interests." The small-state senator sees himself as working in a context dominated by rural-agricultural interests. He cannot escape "a specialty." "In [my state]," he says, "we either farm or we farm the farmers." And he sees no microcosm. He speaks, instead, about the uniqueness of his state, historically, culturally, and environmentally. As for cultivating it, he says, "When they accept you as family, it's easy." To observe senators at home is to become acutely aware that the observation of politicians does indeed, involve "this person in this context." The constituency context, is of course, only an example.

The second large lesson of observation also derives from a basic condition of the research mode. Because you are an outsider in every encounter, and because of the accompanying problems of access, observation is always episodic, never continuous. Your research is, by nature, drop-in-drop-out-drop-in-again research. Your observations get made at irregular intervals and at numerous points in time. You are driven by that condition to an extra appreciation of time. You see not only "this person in this context," but "this person at this time." Attention to time leads, in turn, to an emphasis on the changes that take place over time. Contexts change. And observations made "at this time" will likely differ from those made "last time" or "next time." Finally, any set of serial observations produces a special sensitivity to the sequential aspects of change. Your observation "this time" is embedded in a sequence of "other times." Much of what is important about time and change can be captured in the study of sequences. Some observed sequences exhibit regularities; they seem to have a causal logic to them. They are the most easily and advantageously studied. But random sequences can be observed and studied, too. In sum, the observation of politicians brings with it a sharpened sensitivity to *sequence* as a variable in political analysis.

Observation in the constituency also drives home the importance of sequence. My first encounter with each senator took place in the middle of an election campaign. To observe a campaign is to observe constant change. Contributions, poll results, organizational arrangements, staff, schedules, opposition activities, expectations, media treatment, the candidate's mind—all these ingredients change. The campaign you see in January is not the same campaign you see in the summer, or after Labor Day, or on November 1. Indeed, the campaign you see on the day you arrive is often not the campaign you see on the day you leave. And that is exactly the way campaigners themselves perceive it. They talk to you about the campaign in the language of time, and of change, and of sequence. They speak of stages and phases, of rhythms and flows, of plans and turning points, of gains and losses, of momentum and pace, of beginning games and end games. Campaigns, for all their improvisation, exhibit a good deal of sequential regularity. At the external, public reaction level there is a sequence involving credibility, expectations, and momentum. These sequences can be studied; and so can the random shocks that often alter them. Again, the campaign sequence is only a convenient example.

If, then, the activity of observing politicians has any "value added," it begins with the special sensitivity observation brings to context and to sequence. Politics is a contextual activity and a sequential activity. Students of politics must be students of context and of sequence. Students of American legislative politics need no reminders of the importance of context or sequence—much less of the importance of constituencies and campaigns. To some degree, then, the large lessons to be drawn from observation will simply reenforce ongoing research, and my remarks will add to the chorus. That is fine, for I do not wish to add to the number of variables we treat; I only wish to argue for the richest possible understanding of some we already recognize as central. Here I would like to push a little. For it does not follow from the recognition that context and sequence are important, that they will be given due weight in our research. And it is precisely in the matter of due weight that the observational perspective can be most helpful.

Consider the constituency as context. Its importance for legislative politics is taken to be fundamental and indisputable. One would be hard-put to find a study in the entire field that does not include some mention of the constituency. Yet one would be equally hard-put to find a single constituency anywhere in the United States whose complexity in terms of "this politician in this context" and "at this time" has been analyzed by a political scientist. We love our constituencies, but we do not study them—not up close, in detail, and over time. Can we be satisfied that we know enough about the process by which politicians get recruited and then accumulate (or dissipate) name recognition, reputation, and trust, bit by bit, in multiple intraconstituency contexts over time, when we have yet to study that process for any legislator?

The same can be said for campaigns as sequence. We generalize about them often. But one would be hard-put to find any legislator's campaign for which its yearly, monthly, weekly, even daily sequences have been analyzed up close in detail and over time. Can we be satisfied that we know enough about the ways in which strategic options open up and close down over the course of the campaign, or about the kinds of choices that lead a campaign down one path rather than another, or about the choice points at which such branching decisions get made, when we have yet to follow a single campaign from start to finish? With so little closely detailed investigation of so common a context as the constituency and so common a sequence as a campaign, it seems unlikely that we have yet given these variables the close, hard study they deserve.

From an observational perspective, then, there remains plenty of room for some finely grained, finely calibrated studies of context and of sequence. The observational mode is well suited to such studies. And, indeed, that is the direction in which the close personal observation of politicians will inevitably take us. It is a direction in which we could usefully go. In generalizing about the actions and interpretations of our politicians, we must specify, with the greatest care, the conditions under which each generalization holds. Context and sequence are two such conditions. Perhaps we can draw precise specifications of these conditions without undertaking fairly microscopic analyzes of them. But I doubt it.

I would extend the argument to the other master context in which all legislative politicians work. That is the capital city, where the central activity is governing. Students of legislative politics have given a great deal of attention to the activity of governing and to its sequential patterns, fixed as they are by the formal rules of the legislative process. Here, in our case studies of "how a bill becomes a law," can be found the most numerous examples of scholarly observation. And they have been of enormous value to us. But I should like to push a little here, too. A careful detailing of the perceptions, interpretations, and actions of legislative politicians, developed from the closest possible vantage point, and undertaken with a special sensitivity to context and sequence, can yet improve our understanding of what politicians do in the legislature and why. I shall try to support this argument for "value added" with an extended example.

Decision Making

Ronald Reagan's first foreign policy dispute with the Senate arose over his proposed sale of AWACS planes to Saudi Arabia in the fall of 1981. As governing sequences go, the AWACS controversy was well bounded. By law, the arms sale proposal—the largest in U.S. history—had to be submitted to Congress, where it became subject to a congressional veto if majorities of both houses voted, within 30 days, to disapprove it. The president formally submitted it on October 1 and it was voted on—up or down—by the Senate on October 28. As governing sequences go, also, the AWACS controversy was well publicized. Media interest grew exponentially as the sequence came to its end in the Senate. The House had already voted overwhelmingly to disapprove the sale; the president's prestige and power were thought to be hanging in the balance; the outcome was unpredictable almost until the vote itself. When the vote occurred, every senator was in his or her seat, and every senator voted. It was, thus, a sequence that was easy to follow; and it was a vote about which every senator would have something to say.

Since each of my senators was involved—if only to cast a vote—I talked with them and their staffs about what they saw, what they did, and why. If we think about them in terms of context and sequence, they cluster in three groupings, each group deciding in a different context and at a different point in time. I call them the early deciders, the active players, and the late deciders. I shall discuss two senators from each grouping. And, with apologies, I shall designate them by letter.

Two *early deciders*, both Democrats, were opposed to the sale. They saw themselves, quite simply, as supporters of Israel and of its position.

Accordingly, both committed themselves to that position months before the vote took place. "Basically," said the foreign policy staffer for Senator A, "we were going along with the Israeli position from the beginning.... We signed everything that came along.... Whatever the argument was, we signed on." Because he was a member of the committee of jurisdiction, Senator A was attentive to the issue from its inception. As soon as the administration floated the idea in February, he joined seven committee colleagues in signing a letter to the president expressing "serious" and "deep" concern about the idea and asking the administration to consult with the committee before taking action. In June, he signed a letter circulated by Senator Robert Packwood asking the president not to submit the sale to Congress. And in September, he signed Senator Packwood's official resolution of disapproval on which the eventual vote would be taken.

Viewed from a distance and in the abstract, Senator A expressed an early, strong policy preference, and he voted it. Nothing about his behavior seems problematic. But up close and in context, there are complexities of choice to be observed. Despite his normal activism on foreign policy issues, he made a deliberate decision not to extend his influence beyond the acts of signing and voting in this case. "It was not something we focused on," said his foreign policy aide. "We weren't involved.... We never took an active part in it. The most active we ever got was the senator's statement in committee when the vote came up there.... I wouldn't rank it as one of the biggies we've handled." Senator A did not focus on AWACS because he was preoccupied with other matters at that time. And we are reminded that a strong policy preference does not translate automatically into an equal measure of attention or of involvement.

The timing of Senator A's signature on the formal resolution of disapproval necessitated yet another decision. "We were undecided about signing," explained his staffer, "till late in the summer. Packwood was looking for sponsors even before the hearings were held in committee. [The committee chairman] wanted the members to hold off until they heard the arguments in the committee. We did—until Packwood had gotten into the 40s somewhere, looking for the magic 50 signatures. We didn't want to get in too late, since we had no doubt we'd get in eventually. I remember we discussed it riding in the car. The Senator said 'I don't want to be a Johnny-come-lately.' So we jumped in." And Senator A became number 47 out of the eventual 50 cosponsors. The content of his decision was never in doubt. But the timing of his decision was calculated so as to make certain he would receive full credit for that decision. He believed he would have lost credit with other supporters of Israel if a 50-car pro-Israel train has left the station without him. Whatever the strength or the content of his policy preferences, therefore,

119

he still had to decide how and when those preferences should be publicly expressed. Decisions about how to vote are separable from decisions about attentiveness, decisions about involvement, and decisions about timing. We have devoted far more energy researching the first kind of decision than the other three. Observation could stimulate a useful corrective.

Senator B also committed early and did not change. Like Senator A, he contributed no more to the process or the outcome than to sign and to vote. Senator B became attentive to the AWACS issue not because of his committee, but because of an early spring trip to the Middle East. "Not long after my trip," he said, "someone at home asked me what I thought about AWACS. I said I was against it." Like Senator A, he interpreted the issue as one of support for Israel; and he made his decision in those terms. In his post-trip interview in April with his state's largest paper he said, "This vote could be the most important vote this session, next to the economy. It's a symbolic vote. Where do you stand, with the Arabs or the Jews?"

He was quick to sign both the June Packwood letter and the September Packwood resolution of disapproval. "I was one of the early signers of the Packwood letter," he explained. "I thought that since I had declared a position on the issue, I would become very conspicuous if I did not become a part of the Packwood group." It was the fact of his early commitment more than his policy preference that motivated these actions. And it continued to do so. "I can't say I didn't have second thoughts about it.... I never had that anti-Saudi feeling that Packwood had. I'm not sure why I committed so early. But once I did, I felt I should stay to the end." Near the end, the president invited Senator B to the White House for a chat. He went. "They must have thought they saw a soft underbelly," he said, "that they would say, 'Senator, you've just got to support the president.' One of the deficits a politician can get is to be known as a flip-flopper. So I said to myself, You'll just have to ride this one out." Which he did. "I told the president that I would shed no tears if he won, but that I could not change."

Once again, at a distance and in the abstract, Senator B's behavior is quite straightforward. He expressed a policy preference early and strongly, and he voted it. But observation up close and in sequence reveals something more complex. The strength of his commitment bore little relationship to the strength of his policy preference. And his vote can be explained more by the timing of his commitment than by the substance of it. He committed early; and that act constrained every subsequent interpretation and action. He deemed constancy of commitment to be crucial to his success as a politician. And he interpreted the two Packwood initiatives and the presidential chat as situations in which that connection was being tested.

The cases of Senators A and B suggest that the more carefully we study sequence, the more carefully we shall have to study timing. If we are to explain outcomes, who decides when may be as important to know as who decides what. We have devoted more energy to studying policy positioning in space than to studying policy sequencing in time. To our rich comprehension of the politics of left, right, and center, we can usefully add an equally rich comprehension of the politics of early, later, and late. Here, too, observation can stimulate a useful corrective.

The cases of A and B suggest, also, that we must think of any politician's goals as mixed, and subject to change. As contexts change and as sequences unfold, the relative importance of goals may change. Senator A's policy goal came to be tempered by that of political success. And Senator B's policy goal gradually gave way to one of political success. Both senators were cultivating professional reputations at home and in Washington. Each acted so as to protect that reputation—A so as not to be known as a "Johnny-come-lately," B so as not to be known as a "flip-flopper." These interpretations and actions suggest the supreme importance politicians attach to their reputations. They suggest, too, that the cultivation and protection of favorable reputations involve favorable balances of credit and blame. The pursuit of favorable reputations and favorable credit/blame balances can usually be studied by observation.

Senators C and D, two *active players*, interpreted and acted very differently from Senators A and B. First, they deliberately decided to exert an influence on the outcome beyond their signatures and votes. Second, while both thought of themselves as staunch supporters of Israel, neither interpreted the issue in simple "for or against Israel" terms. Third, because they wanted to maintain negotiating flexibility, they did not commit themselves until much later than A or B. Fourth, by postponing their commitments, they became active in an altered context. In the spring there was much position taking, as with A and B, but no negotiating. In the late summer and early fall, Washington wisdom held that the Senate would disapprove the sale; and that expectation created a context in which the administration had incentives to negotiate—which they did, first with Senator C, later with Senator D.

Senator C, a Democrat, focused on AWACS because, as a member of the committee of jurisdiction, he had long been involved in the problem of arms sales. He possessed a widely acknowledged expertise and commanded much collegial respect in that field. He had developed strong policy preferences. During most of his involvement, these policy goals guided his actions. His pivotal concern was that the AWACS technology not fall into unfriendly hands. His solution was to have the planes flown by joint U.S.-Saudi Arabian crews, and he worked to negotiate a change along these lines prior to the administration's formal submittal. His proposals attracted the support of other senators.

He described his influence in the language of sequence:
> I was involved in it all the way through, but my maximum involvement came early. I was light years ahead of anyone in the Senate when AWACS came up.... From the beginning, I understood what the problem was and I had strong views about it. I believed that wherever that plane went—that very sophisticated piece of technology—our people should go too. I'd say 25 to 28 senators came to me early on to ask for my views. I sat down with each of them for half an hour and talked to them in detail. At this time, I think I had quite a bit of influence on a lot of people's thinking.

His influence came from his ability to redefine the issue and, for a time, to persuade others to focus on his definition of the issue—in this case, the willingness of the Saudis to accept joint Saudi-U.S. crews on the planes. In mid-September Senator C participated, for a few days, in intensive conversations with Senate leaders, with administration officials, and with Saudi representatives. At one point he thought he had brokered, at a meeting in his office, an agreement on joint crewing. But the Saudi government said it would not accept any such arrangement; the administration decided not to push the Saudis, and two days later the proposed sale was formally submitted to the Senate unchanged. "We had an agreement we thought would save the world," said Senator C, "but it turned to worms overnight." And the context of negotiation changed accordingly.

Senator C quickly broke off his negotiating relationship with the White House—largely on the grounds that the Saudi-U.S. actions had rendered his policy goals unattainable. The administration asked him to continue negotiating. But with the demise of his most preferred policy, another personal goal entered his calculation. Senator C wanted to be president of the United States. He feared that any future negotiations would be conducted on the administration's terms, and that he might be "set up" by them to get none of the credit and much of the blame if the sale went through—blame from American Jews that no Democratic hopeful could withstand. As in the earlier cases, changing contexts changed the mix of goals; and strategic calculations were heavily weighted with expectations concerning credit and blame.

When Senator C broke off negotiations, other negotiators entered the picture. Senator D was one of them. And he saw the world very differently from Senator C. Senator D was a Republican. He was a first-year senator. He had no recognized expertise. He had never visited the Middle East. He was not a member of the committee of jurisdiction. He did not have strong policy preferences. But he had a high priority goal. "I want to be known as an effective senator," he said. To that end, he wanted to start, as he put it, "getting involved in the issues, taking some initiatives, doing the work, and getting things accomplished." And he had a lot of energy. AWACS became his proving ground. "[It] took more time than anything else I did this year," he said later. He focused on AWACS partly because "I've always been interested in foreign policy," but mostly because "I like the president and I want him to succeed. This is the president's first foreign policy. We don't want him to lose it." A Reagan loyalist, with no presidential ambitions of his own, he was not constrained to negotiate at arm's length like Senator C. And he plunged in.

"When I first read about AWACS," he said, "I was lukewarm toward it.... But I sat here thinking. There must be some way to get this through.... I even went so far as to call my friend George Will, and I asked him, 'George, how do we get the president out of this mess?'" The question at issue was being reinterpreted for yet a third time—from "Are you for or against Israel?" to "How can we get the Saudis to make concessions?" to "How do we get the president out of this mess?" For my senators, at least, this sequence of interpretations ran parallel to a sequence of action.

Senator D went to majority leader Howard Baker and offered to sound out the uncommitted freshman Republicans on Senator C's joint crewing idea. Senator D himself favored some variant on that idea, and he became Baker's liaison with half a dozen freshmen. When the joint crewing notion "turned to worms," Senator D and his first-year colleagues put forward the idea of an informal letter from the president promising adequate safeguards for the technology—a so-called "letter of certification." Senator D drafted that letter, and others in his group worked it over. Five days after the president sent up his proposal, the freshman group met with James Baker in Senator D's office. "We told Baker," he said, "that this was what we needed if we were to go along, that otherwise we would vote against the sale." The negotiation produced "95 percent agreement" on the letter. And the letter, said Senator D, "became the mechanism for winning over doubting senators. Each one would read it, change it a little bit, and put his Hancock on it somewhere." The letter, as signed by the president, enabled Senator D to make a firm commitment and go home to explain it in mid-October. He thinks the letter provided a necessary rationale for three others in his group. So, Senator D got involved and had an impact on the outcome. It was not large, but it was timely and tangible—and it moved him a measurable distance toward his personal reputational goal.

Legislative outcomes, we know, are invariably negotiated outcomes. This brief and episodic observation of a negotiating sequence suggests that negotiations are, like campaigns, a constantly moving stream. The context in which Senator C's early negotiating efforts took place was not the same context in which Senator D's later negotiating efforts took place. With the passage of time comes contextual change. And with contextual change comes new negotiators pursuing different goals, redefining the issue at hand, altering the decision context for others, and, altogether, shaping new coalitional possibilities. For purposes of coalition building, the United States Senate of late September was simply not the same United States Senate that existed in mid-October. That sense of constant motion ought to superintend all our studies of governing. It is a sense that can be sharpened and shaped by observation.

Also the goals of Senators C and D remind us that for every politician, all governing sequences, like all campaign sequences, are embedded within a yet more encompassing sequence. That is the individual's career sequence. Whenever you observe a politician, he or she is at some stage in a career that stretches back in time and reaches forward in time. His behavior can be interpreted from the perspective of the career path that brought him to where he is, and of the career path he expects will take him where he wants to go. In the case of C and D, their long-run aspirations help us understand their short-run interpretations and actions on AWACS: Senator C's desire to be president; Senator D's desire to be an effective senator. Career aspirations, career building, and career sequences are highlighted by observation and can usefully be studied by observation.

Senators E and F, two *late deciders*, were among the very last members to make a final decision. Senator E decided the night before the vote. Senator F decided the afternoon of the vote. Like the two early deciders, they had no extra involvement in the process; like the early deciders, they signed both Packwood initiatives. But unlike the early deciders, E and F changed their position and voted for the sale. They did so in yet another decision context at yet another stage in the decision making sequence. In late October, President Reagan and the presidentially oriented media entered the picture, and together they reinterpreted the issue at hand. An issue revolving about the various conditions of the sale gave way to one concerning the president's ability to conduct foreign policy. As Senator B, reflecting on his presidential chat, put it, "The substantive issue was lost sight of. The question became, 'Are you for or against the president?'" In this latest of interpretive contexts, Republican Senators E and F reconsidered their earlier decision.

For Senator E, it was the media—aided by the president—which refocused his attention on AWACS. "The whole issue changed in the last week or 10 days," he said. "The media began to play it up as a question involving the president's ability to conduct foreign policy.... The media hyped the deal way out of proportion to what it really deserved. But the media hype made you reevaluate your vote. Had it not been for the media hype, the issue would have been strictly the arms sales. And I would have been very comfortable voting against AWACS." His policy preference never changed; it simply became irrelevant to a vote cast on institutional grounds. "It was," he said, "something I felt changing gradually. No one thing brought me to my conclusion." Not even a last minute chat with the president. "I had a very pleasant conversation with the president.... At the end I said, 'Mr. President...I wish I could say I'm with you, but I can't. All I can say is, I'll keep thinking about it.'" The night before the vote he had a two-hour talk with "the political advisor in the family"—his wife. "We made a checklist—zip, zip, zip on one side, zip, zip, zip on the other side. She asked me 'Well, what do you think it adds up to?' And I said, 'It looks like I ought to support the president.'" And he went to the phone to tell Senator Packwood that he could no longer support the disapproval resolution.

Senator E's early commitment was not controlling for him, as it was for Senator B, because, unlike Senator B, he did not believe that his reputation was at stake. With his Senate colleagues, Senator E's reputation was undamaged because his change of position moved him back under the protective cover of his party's majority and of his party's leader. With his constituents, Senator E simply did not believe that his reputation depended on constancy of commitment. "The state media were very good to me," he said afterward. "With them I have established a reputation as someone who is independent, who does as he goddamned pleases, who can't be pushed around. That helps. It gives you room to case a vote like this without people saying you've been had. It's not easy to climb down from your position and take another one in the full glare of national publicity. But the state media treated me like I knew what I was doing." While all politicians act so as to cultivate and protect their professional reputations, how they go about it depends not only on the reputation they want, but on what they think their reputation already is. That crucial matter of perception and interpretation can be studied by observation.

There are nearly as many reasons why senators pay attention to a problem as there are senators. It was committee membership for A, a trip for B, expertise for C, a desire to help the president for D, the media for E. We need to know what these stimuli are if we are to understand the subsequent involvement, interpretation, and action of each individual politician. For Senator F, conversations with Israeli friends triggered his reevaluation. He thought long and hard about the problem, and the immense pressures he felt on the day of the debate were self-generated.

He had a strong attachment to Israel; but he gradually became convinced that Israel might be just as well off with the sale as without it. "The more I looked at it," he said, "the more I began to worry about what the situation would look like if the deal did not go through—the Saudis with their hurt pride, the British in there selling the Saudis the same weapons, Israel asking us for arms to control the Saudis, Israel blamed for the defeat of the sale, and a president who had his wings clipped in his first foreign policy effort. As bad as the sale was for Israel, I began to think the defeat of it might be worse." He found that most of his Israeli friends agreed with him. He did not reinterpret the question in institutional, "for or against the president" terms as E had done. Senator F's preferred policy changed because he took in more information relevant to his original question—the effect on Israel. His preference changed because his information had changed. Either way, through the imposition of a new issue or through the addition of information on the old issue, preferences can change as the governing sequence unfolds. Thus we are reminded that the sequence itself has an autonomous effect on the politicians involved in it. And it must be studied as such. Observation at close range is well suited to studying this impact of processes on outcomes.

On the eve of the vote, Senator F was leaning but undecided. "I stayed up all night before writing a pro-AWACS speech. But I still was not certain how I was going to vote.... Up until 10 minutes before I gave my speech I honestly wasn't certain what I was going to do." His course of action was finally fixed by a confluence of context and of sequence. He found himself in a situation in which he could cast the deciding vote for the sale, and he consciously did so. "A little after noon," he said, "I went to Howard Baker and I asked him what his count was. He said, 'Forty-nine.' I asked, 'What about X?' He said, 'He won't talk to anyone.' I asked, 'How about Y?' He said, 'We can't get to him.'" "I was the only one they could count on,..." explained F. And he added, "If the sale was going through, and if I could be the fiftieth vote, then I could exert more leverage with the administration and be in a better position to help Israel.... Conversely, I didn't want some oil state senator to be the fiftieth vote." The sale went through, 52 to 48.

On his credit/blame balance sheet, Senator F got the worst of both worlds. Supporters of Israel assumed his was the decisive vote; and they blamed him for their loss. "I got more flak from that vote by far than any I have ever cast in the Senate," he said later. And supporters of AWACS gave him no credit for their victory. Three years afterward he said, "Do you know, the administration never thanked me for helping them on the vote, never gave me anything, never acknowledged that I helped them." So much for our abstract generalizations about the special benefits accruing to the latest deciding, pivotal voters. In the concrete, it seems, there are interpretive contingencies to be reckoned with. You are pivotal only if the distributors of credit and blame think you are, and politicians understand that condition. Thus, the allocation, as well as the creation, of credit and blame, should be studied—and they can both be studied by observation.

Conclusion

It should not be thought that I have told *the* story of AWACS. Far from it. At best I have told six little stories to feed into the larger story of AWACS. But the six stories suggest how complex *the* story of any large legislative decision must be, and how many different decision contexts and decision sequences are involved. They further suggest how much research room yet remains for the microscopic, observation-based analyses of the governing activity of legislative politicians. If, that is, such analyses have value. I have tried to make the case, by example, that they do.

The stories of decision making by six senators suggest that observation can be an aid to discovery, description, and theorizing. They further suggest that this "value added" flows from a heightened sensitivity to context and to sequence. In these briefest of discussions—about such analytic foci as attentiveness, involvement, and timing in decision making; or about changing contextual impacts on decision making; or about calculations concerning goals, reputations, and credit/blame balances; or about interpretive sequences, negotiating sequences, voting sequences, and career sequences—there is, I would argue, sufficient warrant for the claims of observation. These claims have been stated in incremental language, as befits the notion of "value added," to wit: "sensitize," "emphasize," "suggest," "remind," "correct," "stimulate," "aid," "improve," "highlight." But in research involving politicians, these modest claims may represent an indispensable increment of knowledge and understanding.

Given the benefits of direct observation, two questions remain. Do we need political scientists to do it? And if we do, are enough political scientists doing it?

As for the first question, there is a huge corps of journalists who observe politics every day. They do it very well. We are already heavily dependent on what they tell us about our politicians. If we do not do it, they will do it for us. But it is in the nature of their occupation that they have neither the training, nor the patience, nor the interest to conduct a dialogue with political science theorizers. Journalists are not conceptualizers or generalizers. They are more interested in episodes than regularities. Their observations are not driven by the questions of political science. Put it this way, if my observations are interchangeable with those of a journalist, then I shall desist. If not, I shall argue that we cannot leave the field to the journalists, that we need political scientists to go take a first-hand look at our politicians and report back to us. We need political scientists to keep doing it. For only we can persist in attaching observation to theory. Surely, we cannot construct theories of politics on the basis of observation. But we might ask ourselves whether it is possible to construct theories of politics without observational perspectives—if we wish our theories to encompass the serious activity of our politicians.

As for the second question, I believe that not enough political scientists are presently engaged in observation. Unless I misread our journals, our graduate methods courses, and our reward structure in general, young political scientists have little incentive to expend time and energy observing politicians. Observation-based research is a rarity in the *American Political Science Review*. There are many reasons for this; each of them may be valid in its own terms. But the question is a disciplinary one. How much value do we place on observation as a research mode? How much legitimacy do we wish to bestow on observation-based research? Have we tried our very best to teach observation and failed? Or have we made a standing decision against its claims of added value to us? We shall not answer these questions until we examine them with care. Perhaps, sometime and somehow, that careful examination will take place within the political science profession. I hope so.

Index